GETTING READY TO WRITE

Exploring all the crucial development stages before children even pick up a pencil

Published 2013 by Featherstone, an imprint of Bloomsbury Publishing plc,
50 Bedford Square,
London,
WC1B 3DP
www.bloomsbury.com

ISBN 978-1-4081-9318-1

Printed in Great Britain by Latimer Trend & Company Ltd

10 9 8 7 6 5 4 3 2 1

This book is produced using paper that is made from wood grown in managed, sustainable forests. It is natural, renewable and recyclable. The logging and manufacturing processes conform to the environmental regulations of the country of origin.

To see our full range of titles visit **www.bloomsbury.com**

Acknowledgements
Many thanks to LEYF for their kind permission to reproduce photographs.
We would like to thank the staff and children of the following settings:
Penguin Pre School
The Arches Primary School
Middlefield Primary School
Saint Augustines RC Primary School
St Thomas More Primary School
Noahs Ark Pre School
Woodhouse Primary School
Halton Lodge Primary School
The Friars Primary School
Crofton Hammond Infant School
Hinguar Primary and Nursery School

Contents

Introduction

As a classroom teacher trying to get children in reception to write, I think I probably got more things wrong than I did right. It wasn't that the children that I taught never learnt to write, far from it. But looking back, given what I now know and understand, I think I could have done so much better, especially for those children who were reluctant mark makers and writers. What my teaching suffered from was a combination of lack of knowledge, inappropriate practice and pressure to get children writing as soon as possible.

Once you begin to understand the physical development of mark making and combine that with children's phonological awareness and engagement, then you have got a winning combination.

First of all, let's consider the physical aspect of the mark making journey and try and make some sense out of that. If we trace our ancestry back to the time of the evolution of our species, we find ourselves in the company of primitive man (and woman). While they were discovering how to make fire and build shelters do you think that primitive man said 'I am just popping out to catch our tea' and primitive woman replied 'Hold on, I need a few bits while you are out. I will write you a list!' Of course not!

Being able to write is not a fundamental need that our bodies are designed for. We have evolved a physical body that enables us to survive as a hunter-gatherer. So all of the physical movements that our body is accomplished at doing are there because we need them to be able to survive.

We have tiny pivots at the ends of our fingers as well as at our knuckles, wrists, elbows and shoulders: these provide us with a huge range of motion from the ability to pick up tiny objects to powerful throwing actions. Our palms enable us to grasp, hold and control a range of tools for a variety of uses. Our feet are flat on the floor to help us to balance while we use this range of motion on our upper body. Meanwhile our brain, assisted by our senses, is constantly working to help us to process all the information that we are taking in. This enables us to balance, judge distance, move appropriately in the space that we have (proprioception) and select the right bits of our body to do the job that needs to be done.

Whereas our distant ancestors might have used their hands to make flint arrow heads, skin animals or sharpen sticks, we now use them to help us to communicate through mark making and writing. We are not born as writers. The physical ability to write requires great dexterity and muscle control, which in turn takes practice.

If we want children to be enabled and successful writers then it really helps if we are able to understand the small step stages of physical development and dexterity, how they link into mark making and what we can do on a daily basis to support and extend children in their progress.

Alongside this essential physical development we also need to give children a huge range of experiences to help them to grow their imagination, lots of quality talk to give them the vocabulary and the language mechanisms of writing plus a healthy dollop of phonics to enable them to record their talk in ways that can be understood.

There are a number of day to day elements of your practice that could impact on this development.

Knowledge

Hopefully, by reading this you will learn some things that will have a positive impact on your children's development and also you will be more aware of the areas of development that you might want to look into and investigate further.

Assessment

It is essential that you assess your children not only by the letter sounds that they know but also by their stage of physical development both in their upper body and their grip. Once you are aware of where they are at, then you can identify next steps for their development.

Environment

Following good assessment you will then need to show how you are reflecting that assessment in your environment. If you have identified a group of children who are still using really gross motor upper body movements then where have you made provision available for them? By the same token if you have a group of children who are using very fine motor movements where is your provision for them?

Challenge

Once your assessment is complete and you have put provision in place to reflect the needs that you have identified, then you have the eternal dilemma of how you get the children you have targeted to use the correct resources. Also how are you showing that the resources you have put out are taking these children's learning forward and not just creating opportunities for low level non challenging play?

The classic scenario is the reception child (usually a girl) who walks into the mark making area and selects some white paper and felt tips and produces this type of work in about a minute and a half.

It is very good with lots of detail and shows a high level of dexterity. As an adult you might be tempted to 'ooh' and 'ahh' over it, but actually in terms of learning and challenge this child is only consolidating a skill that she is already good at. There is nothing in that area to move her forward. If she does that every time she goes into the mark making area then a great deal of her time will be spent in learning stagnation.

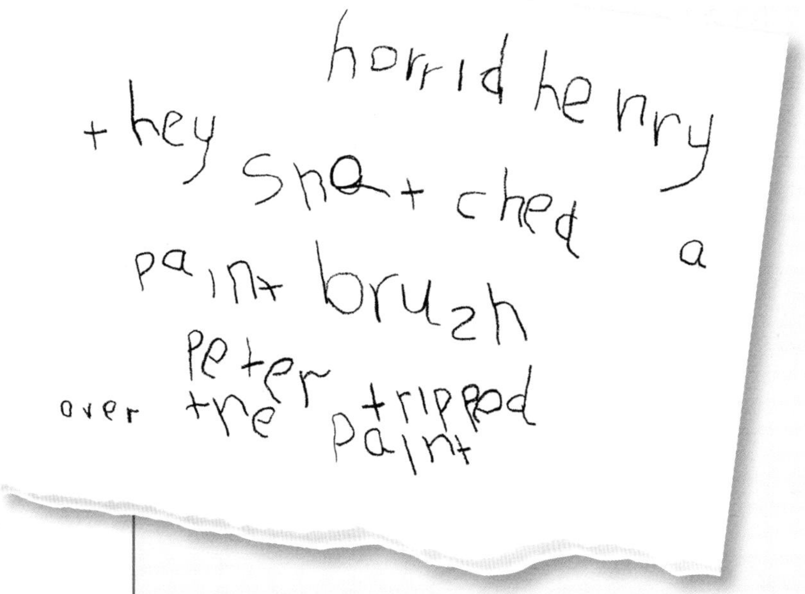

Continuous Provision

We have to stop thinking about continuous provision as 'the stuff we always have out' and start thinking about it as 'continuing the provision for learning in the absence of an adult'. That is when continuous provision will actually have an impact on learning. You cannot guarantee what a child will do in an area when you are not there with them to support and guide their play. But, you can show that all areas of your continuous provision are linked to assessment, resourced to reflect needs that you have identified through assessment and observation and then dressed to engage children in subject areas in which they are interested. Do you have resources that develop all the stages of mark making and writing all of the time?

Timetable

Children not only need opportunities to develop their skills through continuous provision they also need direct adult input on a daily basis. If a child can has a choice between something that they can already do and that they find easy or something that is hard and going to challenge them, they will always pick the easy option! Therefore some regular, quality adult intervention with high levels of engagement can really move children's progress on quickly, rather than waiting for it to happen by chance. A great deal of mark making attainment comes from the children's ability to develop and control their muscles. If we wanted to develop our muscles quickly then we would do exercise every day and work on specific areas that we wanted to improve. We should apply the same principle to children's physical development for writing.

Chapter 1

Upper body

When children first begin to mark make they are not doing it necessarily to convey meaning, they are doing it because they can. How children use their body to aid their early mark making and then writing is by using a sequence of muscle movements. Which muscles they use depends on their stage of development. Most children follow the same sequence of development, so once you are aware of it you are able to assess where your children are and create an appropriate environment to support and extend them.

Shoulder pivot

During the early stages of development, when children are learning to support their head, reach, grasp, and walk they are using groups of muscles in their pelvis, back, shoulders, arms and neck. It is these upper body muscle groups that they use in the very emergent stages of mark making.

Children will have already developed a grasp that allows them to hold something tight without dropping it. This grasp is formed by wrapping the fingers around the object and making a fist with the object held in the middle: this is known as a 'palmer supinate grasp' ('palmer' from the use of the palm, 'supinate' meaning turning the palm upwards and 'grasp' meaning grip). This is the grip that children most commonly employ in early mark making.

At this stage in their development, the muscles of their upper body that are the most well developed are the neck, chest and back. It is these muscles that have the most strength, so it is these muscles that are used to help the hand to make those first emergent marks. Often at this stage the child will have a fairly stiff wrist and a straight elbow with most of the movement coming from the shoulder. The type of mark that a child at this stage of development can make will be at the maximum range, so they are likely to be long and straight or large and circular as their range of movement is restricted to the strongest muscle group they have available.

As part of your assessment for mark making are you looking for children who are pivoting from the shoulder with a palmer supinate grasp? Once you have identified those children can you show how you have created areas of your provision, both indoors and out that will consolidate and further develop that range of movement to move it onto the next stage of development?

Within your planning for adult-led activities, can you show how you have grouped children for specific interventions and also how you will support their mark making development during periods of child-led learning or continuous provision?

Supporting and extending a shoulder pivot

Children using this pivot are employing the full range of motion of their arm so they therefore need large spaces to be able to mark make where that full motion can be accommodated.

Large boards at child height are ideal for this range of movement, plus they will support all of the other stages as well. It is a good idea to have these large scale boards both indoors and out. They needn't be expensive: you can coat large sheets of ply wood with blackboard paint to make very large and versatile mark making boards. If you are going to use these boards outside then choose marine ply or outdoor ply as this has been pre-treated and will not rot.

Variety is indeed the spice of life when it comes to engagement for mark making so try and have as many different types of surface as you can for the children to experiment on. Alongside your chalk boards you can also use large whiteboards, sheets of Perspex and also plastic mirrors to give a range of different experiences.

Remember that children will want to mark make in every area of your environment so opportunities for this gross motor movement should be available in every area. If your paint easels are only A3 size then they are not allowing for this provision. Also, alongside gross and fine motor development we want to encourage lots of talk for writing so as many areas as you can need to be flexible to support individual work, but also encourage collaboration. On a small board or a small easel you can only fit one child and their work; on a larger space you have the option to work alone or as part of a group.

Proprioception and balance

Alongside the development of their upper body muscles, children are also developing their sense of proprioception and balance. Proprioception is the brain using all sorts of information from different parts of the body to help it to move effectively within its given space. An essential part of this movement is being able to maintain balance while still and also in motion. Large physical movements of the arms and upper body shift the centre of balance and so continually challenge the child's sense of proprioception, sometimes resulting in a child falling over.

Upside down mark making

If a child is lying on their back with their arm extended up above them to make a mark, it is the same upper body movement as if they are standing in front of a board. By asking children to lie on their back you will get an added element of engagement so try a bit of 'upside down' writing where you attach large pieces of paper to the bottom of tables and get the children to slide in on their backs and mark make. Cover the table with a cloth and throw in a couple of torches and you will have them queuing up for a turn!

Upper body work out

Once we have established that we are concentrating on developing children's shoulder movement and their sense of proprioception then we can plan for fixed or permanent structures in our environment to support this movement as well as activities to support it. The activities that we plan will involve the use of the shoulder pivot on both horizontal and vertical surfaces. The activity will encourage the children to reach and stretch as well as use the full circular motion of their shoulder joint. For children who you know are at this stage of development you would engage them in this type of activity on a daily basis.

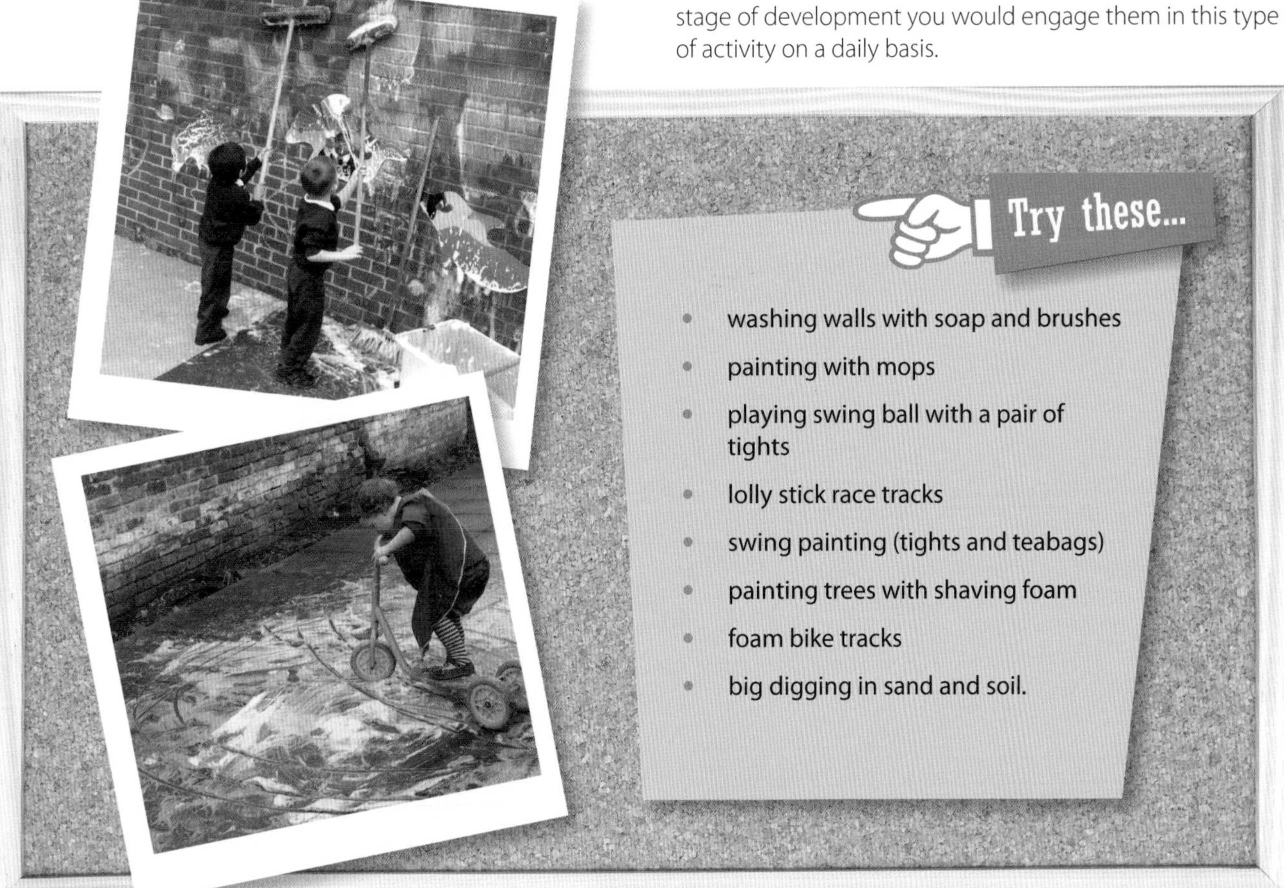

Elbow pivot

Once the muscles in the back, upper arms and shoulders begin to strengthen there usually starts to be more movement further down the arm at the next point of pivot: the elbow. At this stage in development the shoulder becomes more sedentary and the elbows start to do more of the work. There are usually two noticeable stages in the elbow pivot: the first is the 'emergent' stage where the elbow bends allowing for a greater range of movement, but the shoulder is still the main 'power' in moving the arm backwards and forwards. This looks like a sawing motion where the arm tends to move in straight lines across the body or from front to back.

Secondly, when a child becomes more proficient in their elbow pivot then they begin to use the muscles in their upper and lower arm to swing their arm in and out from their body in a semi-circular action, thus significantly increasing their range of movement. Often when the elbow pivot is developing, the wrist stays quite stiff and the grip is still palmer supinate.

As with a shoulder pivot, when you are assessing children's mark making abilities and planning their next steps for development then you need to know when they have reached this stage and what you have purposefully put in your provision and planning to consolidate that skill and take them forward.

Supporting and extending an elbow pivot

First of all you need to split your children into 'emergent' and 'proficient' elbow pivoters because you will promote different activities for each. For 'emergent' children you really want to encourage them to use their full range of motion but, bending their elbows. You are going to need lots of space for them to move their arms up and down as well as from side to side across their body.

Using large rollers or brushes up and down on outside surfaces is not only good for developing the elbow pivot but will also consolidate the shoulder pivot and support ongoing development of balance and proprioception.

A sweeping motion with a stiff outside brush is also good for this elbow pivot. The children can have sweeping races through piles of leaves or create foam tracks on a rainy day with the aid of some washing-up liquid!

It is really important, indoors and out, to have some large spaces to support this range of movement. Often we might cover a table top in plain paper and leave that as continuous provision for mark making. This is great for the first few children who 'have a go' but once the paper begins to fill then some children will not visit the activity because it doesn't offer them the 'clean' spaces to make the marks that they are looking for. So try and have a regular supply of clean paper available that the children can self manage, allowing adults in the setting to do less housekeeping and more targeted intervention for learning.

Good old blackboard paint is a lifesaver here too. You can not only paint boards with it but you can also paint your walls and furniture. This photograph shows a very inexpensive table from a well known Swedish furniture retailer that has been painted all over (including underneath) with blackboard paint allowing children to literally chalk all over it.

It is worth leaving a damp cloth on hand and/or a misting spray bottle that the children can use to clean the table before they use it. The motion of the cleaning will also target the development that you are concentrating on and a damp surface will make the chalk appear very different, which may present some great opportunities for language development.

You can also purchase 'blackboard oilcloth' which is exactly that: oilcloth which can be chalked on like a blackboard. This can be laid on a table top, secured to the floor and walls, taped around the trunk of a tree ... the possibilities are endless!

In this photograph the child is developing an emergent elbow pivot by sawing wood with a hacksaw. It is not the opportunity to develop his elbow pivot that has attracted him to this activity, more the opportunity to get his hands on a saw. It worked a treat.

For a more secure elbow pivot, you really want the children to develop that circular 'push/pull' movement with their upper and lower arm. There are lots of activities that you can do that involve a circular motion, both large and small. It can be something as simple as drawing circles onto large sheets of sugar paper and you can try doing this to music for an extra bit of inspiration.

You can also link this sort of activity to children's interests. These boys are using a large lolly stick turned onto its side to 'clear' a circular track to race their cars on. If you make a track into a 'figure eight' then you will be developing their shoulder and elbow pivot, and also introducing the children to a wrist pivoting movement.

You can add sequins and glitter to the sand tray so it could also be used for making much smaller and finer lolly stick patterns with a group of children who are developing their fine motor grip.

This group of boys are inspired by Super Mario and are developing that more advanced elbow pivot by mixing pizza dough (flour and water paste)! Add more water for an easier mixing experience and more flour to really challenge them.

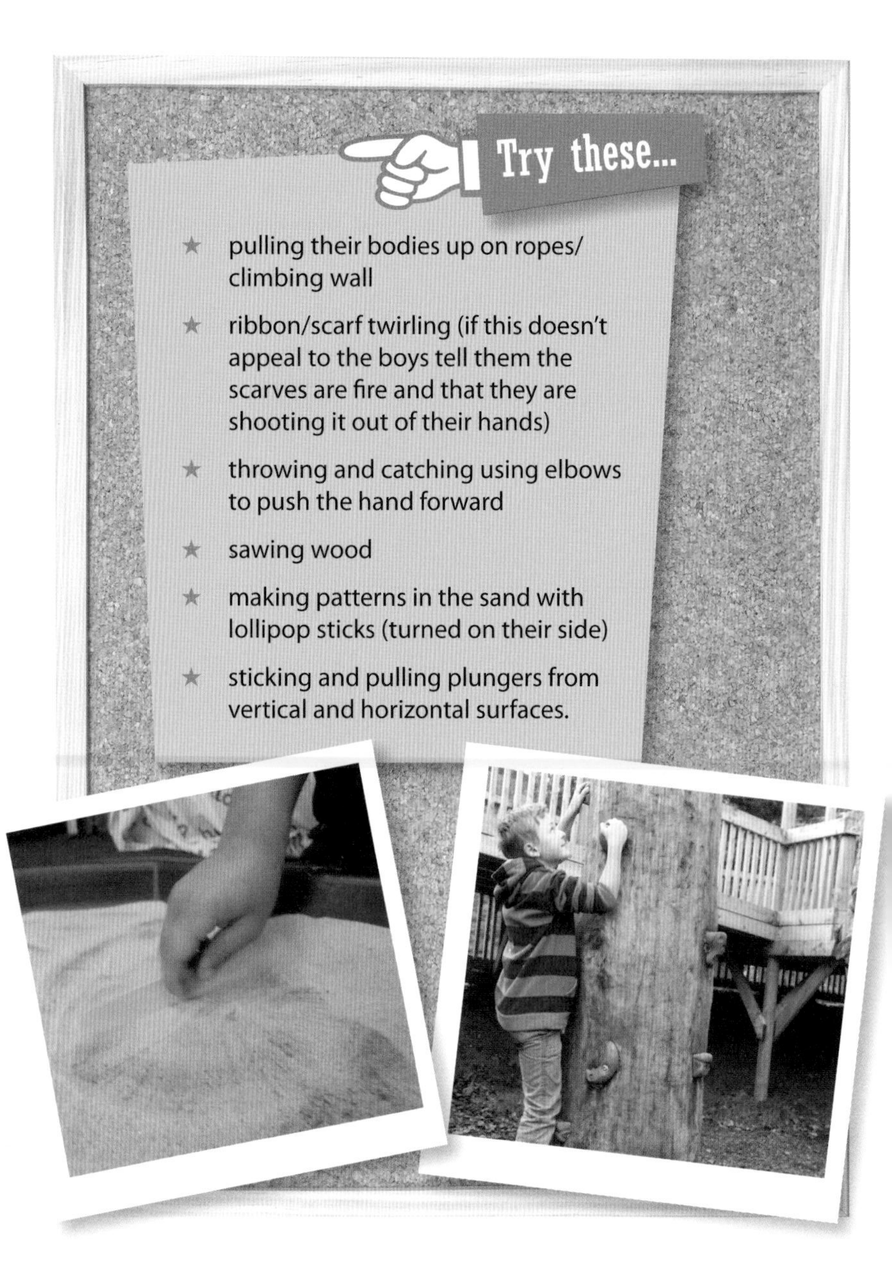

Wrist pivot

As the arm muscles and the sense of balance develop further then the pivot changes again, this time to allow an even smaller range of movement. This time the pivot moves to the wrist. The elbow often tucks in to the side of the body and the shoulder movement is now minimal.

By the time that children reach the wrist pivot stage in their development their lower arms, upper arms and shoulders are all now well developed and their overall movement and balance tends to be far more fluid than it was when they first started out on this journey of development. The wrist pivot stage is the one that children tend to stick with for the least amount of time before their pivot shifts again.

Often with a wrist pivot comes a change in a child's grip from palmer supinate to digital pronate ('digit' meaning finger and 'pronate' meaning to grasp with the palm turned down).

When a child adopts a digital pronate grip they bend their wrist to nearly 45°, grip their mark making implement with three fingers and use their first finger to manipulate the end of their pencil.

This is a clear sign that their stage of fine motor manipulation is moving forward and also an indicator that we need to be looking out for and encouraging the next stage of development both in pivot and grip.

Supporting and extending a wrist pivot

When planning provision to support a developing wrist pivot we want to encourage the whole range of wrist movement. The wrist pivot itself is allowing the child a much more defined and small scale range of movement (as well as the larger elbow and shoulder movement). It is the palm grip that now restricts the child's access to this finer range of movement which is why this pivot often signals that move in grip (although not always).

The overall movement of the activities that you plan for a developing wrist pivot will be much smaller in their range than you have planned before. You might want to reduce everything in size to encourage the child to really focus on their development.

If they are drawing or painting you could give the children thin strips of paper that could be painted either vertically or horizontally: don't make them too large in size or it will encourage them to use their elbow and their shoulder to create large sweeping motions. If you keep the pieces of paper thin and relatively short the children will have gone from the beginning to the end of the paper, using their wrist, before there is time or space for their other, more well developed, pivots to kick in.

Having a range of smaller working surfaces constantly available for the children to self select is always a good idea. You can paint cheap painting canvasses with blackboard paint and fasten them to the back of a low level display with 'Velcro'. The children can access them independently, mark make on them and then return them to their ready-made gallery.

Any sort of threading or weaving activity is great for developing a wrist pivot. However, the thing about threading is that it has great benefits but is essentially dull, especially for those children who would rather be playing more adventurous games outside. It is not often that you will see those children whoop with joy at the sight of some plastic cotton reels! So don't just think about which activities get the children flexing the right muscles in the right places, think about what is going to make them want to engage with that activity in the first place and consider how you can theme it around their interests.

Chapter 2

Get a grip!

The physical journey that our brain takes us on to become a dexterous mark maker is actually quite straightforward and makes perfect sense. As we have seen, it starts with the nearest 'bendy bit' of arm to where the greatest muscle group is strongest and then works its way down to the next 'bendy bit' once the muscles and balance will support that movement.

Once the pivots have worked their way down to the wrist, the journey doesn't stop there, although for many children it becomes far trickier and this is where they often get stuck.

The end of the 'pivot' journey will be when children get that mark making implement to the very last, smallest set of pivots, right at the end of the fingers. If they can hold their mark making tools there then they will have the fullest, most dexterous range of movement that our bodies can provide.

Fine motor strength

The hand is quite a complex piece of machinery and is made up of lots of different joints and muscle groups that interconnect and work together to provide maximum dexterity. In a child's journey to becoming a mark maker and eventually a writer they need to be proficient in all of the following. When you are thinking about the provision that you have available for developing children's fine motor dexterity it is useful to think about the skill first and then match this to the activity.

Pincer grasp or grip

This enables a child to pick up small items using the thumb and index finger. The most basic form of this skill is when children use all their fingers to 'rake' items into the palm of their hand. During the next phase of their development they might pinch items with the thumb against the side of the index finger before moving on to a more accomplished grip, where they can use the end of their thumb and forefinger in a pincer grasp to manipulate small objects effectively.

Palm arches

There are several arches within the palm of your hand that enable the hand to grasp a range of different objects of various sizes and shapes. These arches direct the skilled movement of your fingers and control the power of your grasp. Your palm arches are directly related to your ability to manipulate a mark making implement (like a pencil or paintbrush). If your palm arches are not well developed then they cannot provide enough support to your fingers to allow them in turn to manipulate the mark making tool. This is why children will grasp their mark making implement in their palm at the earliest stages of their development.

In-hand manipulation

This skill refers to the ability to move and position objects within one hand without the assistance of the other hand. Children (and some adults) often find this really hard. Children need lots of practice with items such as elastic bands and pencils, moving them in between their fingers. Also use round objects like conkers or marbles which they have to rotate in the palm of one hand. Usually with fine motor dexterity exercises you would start with large objects because they are easiest. With in-hand manipulation it is the opposite: the larger the object the more challenge.

Thumb opposition

This refers to the ability to turn and rotate the thumb so that it can touch each fingertip of the same hand. Start with the palm spread and then get the children to use their thumb to touch each of the fingertips in turn. After each individual touch always return to a spread palm. When they become proficient at doing this with each hand individually then get them to do both hands at the same time. To extend this challenge further ask the children to do both hands together, but start with the index finger on one hand and the little finger on the other. This is not only good for developing dexterity, but also bilateral brain work. (Try it, it is harder than you think!)

Finger isolation

To do this you need to be able to move each finger one at a time. At the early stages of dexterity development children will move all of their fingers together in a grasping motion. As they develop, they learn to move the fingers individually. This ability is very important in the development of fine motor skills as it is the mechanism that will allow children to hold and manipulate a pencil or a paintbrush as well as tie laces, push buttons and a host of other everyday essential skills.

Knuckle, PIP and DIP joints

Although this sounds a bit like a children's television programme, it actually refers to the joints in your hand, thumb and fingers. The first one that you come to is the knuckle (or metacarpophalangeal joint). This is usually very flexible and used for grabbing, raking and also in pencil grips like *palmer supinate* (see page 14). The next joint is the proximal interphalangeal joint (the PIP joint) and this is used for all major grips and finger manipulations. The final finger joint is the distal interphalangeal joint (the DIP joint) and this is the one that you need to be able to manipulate well to support a tripod grip. To develop this joint you need to work with things that are small and fiddly and malleable materials that give a high level of resistance.

Bilateral coordination

We all need to be able to coordinate both sides of the body at the same time in a controlled way. This can mean using both sides to do the same thing, like pushing open a door or jumping into a puddle. We also need to be proficient at using alternating movements when both sides of the body are doing the same thing but not at the same time. Walking is a good example of this where our arms and legs will be making a similar movement to each other but in sequence. The most complex level of bilateral coordination is where the body has to do two completely different movements on each side but at the same time, such as cutting with scissors while holding and controlling the paper with the other hand.

Crossing the midline

This skill primarily involves more upper body gross motor movement, rather than the smaller fine motor skills that we are focusing on in this section, but it can have significant impact on children's ability to manipulate objects using their hands. It is the ability to cross your arms and legs over to the other side of your body. Children who are in the early stages of developing this skill would not be able to do things like draw a horizontal line across a page in front of them without changing hands halfway through. It is an important skill because it is used in everything from helping us to read by tracking print from left to right across a page to being able to put our socks on!

Hand-eye coordination

The correct term for this is visual motor integration and it is one of the fundamental skills which holds the key to so many of the things that children need to be able to do, not only to become successful mark makers but to have success in virtually every aspect of their life. This is the ability to control hand movement guided by vision and we use this skill to enable us to draw, paint, thread, cut, pour, eat, build and write – to name but a few. It is essential that children have lots of practice in developing this skill on a daily basis.

This list is not exhaustive but contains the essential skills that children need to evolve before they can become writers. Most of these skills will develop eventually in an environment where children have lots of opportunities to play and explore in a range of situations that challenge both their gross and fine motor development. As practitioners we can play an essential role in supporting and extending that development by ensuring that we have a good depth of knowledge, accurate assessment and observations in place and an environment that reflects the information that our assessment gives us.

Assessing grip development

All children start their mark making journey with a **palmer supinate grip** or palm grip. This is the grip that will probably be prevalent through the entire shoulder, elbow and possibly wrist pivot development. The mark making implement is held in the palm of the hand and the fingers are clamped around it to keep it in place. There is not yet the development in the palm arches or the dexterity in the fingers to support the mark making tool being held in any other way. All of the manipulation and movement of your mark making tool is coming from a pivot further up the arm. Only when the muscles in the arm have been strengthened (and the pivots have moved from shoulder to wrist) alongside mastering the palm arches and the in-hand manipulation skills, will there be enough dexterity and strength to support a grip change.

Palmer supinate grip

This first grip change is likely to be a **digital pronate grasp**, although not all children go through this stage of development. It is called a digital pronate because the children primarily use one digit (finger) to pronate (rotate/manipulate) their mark making implement. To adopt a digital pronate grasp you have to be able to pivot from the wrist as you need to be able to achieve that 90° angle to get to the paper.

Digital pronate grasp

What often comes next is a grip that tends to be more prevalent in boys than girls. This is also a tricky grip because its development often coincides with children's ability to begin to link sounds to letters and record them as recognisable symbols or begin to recognise and write their name. This grip is called the **expanded** or **static tripod grip**. The mark making tool has been pushed right to the end of the fingers. The thumb is used to 'clamp' the mark making tool in place and it is mainly the little finger that is creating the range of movement.

Although this is a perfectly normal stage of mark making development for some children, it is a particularly crucial one and needs to be handled with care! If a child begins to regularly record recognisable letters with this (or any other) unusual grip their brain very soon gets into the habit of thinking that this way of holding their pencil and forming letters is 'comfortable' and it becomes the norm. The more they do it, the more they are embedding this grip and range of movement.

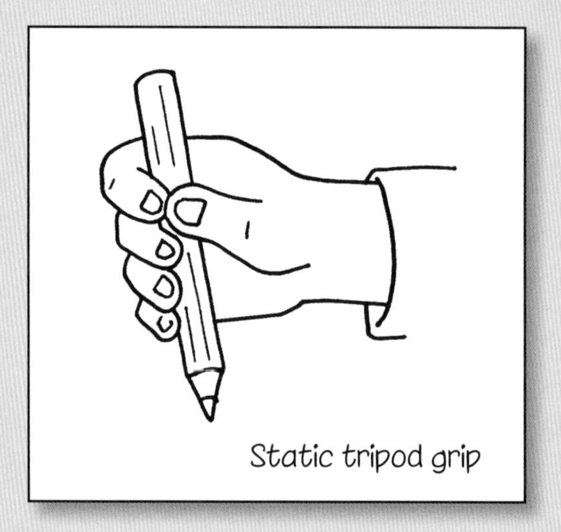
Static tripod grip

Once children have mastered the art of holding their pencil and orientating their letter shapes with the wrong grip it can become almost impossible to get them to change. I know of many children (usually boys) who began to write with the wrong grip and were then put on torturous 'handwriting programmes' to try and correct their grip. The thing is, that they can attempt to triangulate when they are sitting in a handwriting intervention class, but when they get back into the classroom and their brain isn't just thinking about handwriting any longer then it reverts back to its 'norm' and they are back to square one. So, when you see an expanded tripod developing then that is the time to intervene and help children to transition to the 'ultimate' grip: **the triangulation**!

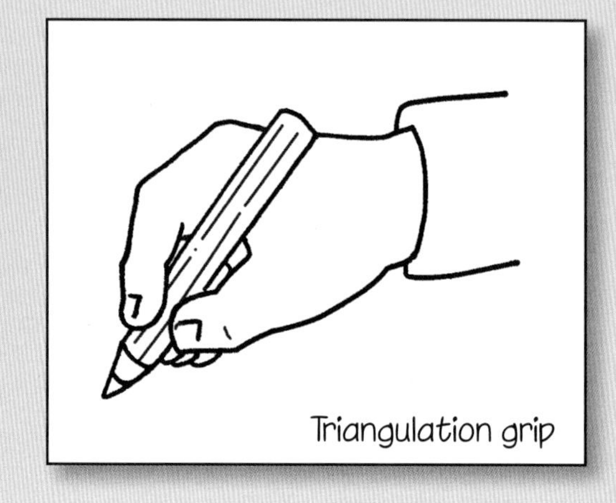
Triangulation grip

Another version of this grip is an **inverted tripod grip** where the child's little finger and fourth finger are behind the pencil near to the point and their index and second finger are curled around the front of it mid way up. Meanwhile their thumb is at the very top of the pencil clamping it in place against the fingers.

Children who adopt an expanded or inverted tripod grip often do this because they still lack dexterity in their final finger joints. These children need lots of opportunity to practise manipulating these joints, either by using them to pick up or manoeuvre tiny objects, or to work with a small amount of malleable material that will give a great deal of resistance like a putty.

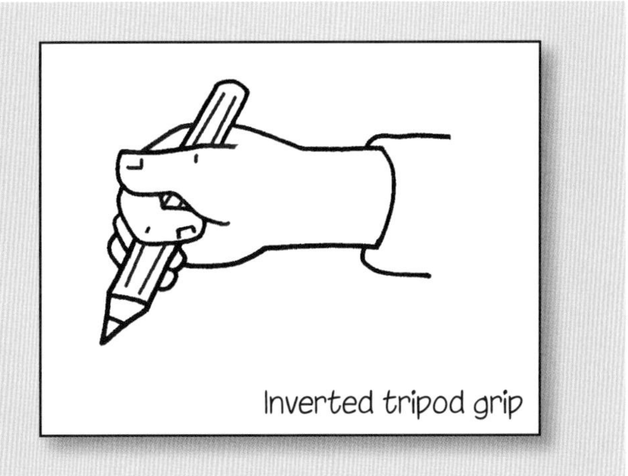
Inverted tripod grip

A **triangulation** or **tripod grip** is where the mark making implement is held between the thumb and the forefinger and supported from behind with the middle finger. The movement of the mark making implement is controlled by the pivoting joints for the thumb and fingers. This allows for maximum flexibility and maximum range of movement and is why it is the 'ultimate grip'!

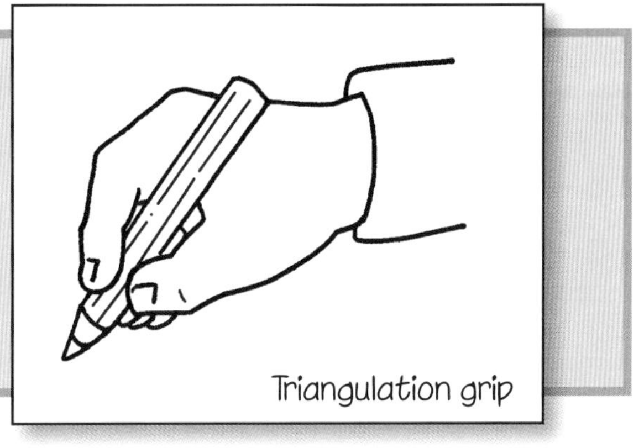
Triangulation grip

Tracking progress

As I have already said, it is really important that you are able to assess and track children's progress in their grip development so that you know that you are putting in place the provision that is required.

Several of the settings that I have worked with have used the images opposite and above to create a visual tracker on their setting wall. As this display is for adult information and not for children you could place it in the space at the top of your walls.

The images can be blown up to A3 size and then on a sticky note match the name of the child to their stage of development. This makes a good visual reminder for adults and you can then move the sticky notes along as the children make progress.

More importantly it will cause you to reflect on the provision that you have made available. Have you got activities and resources in place for all of the stages you have identified?

Chapter 3

Malleable materials

When it comes to getting ready to write, the use of malleable materials really comes into its own. I often find that it is a much maligned and misunderstood area which doesn't really fulfil its purpose. Partly I think this is because lots of practitioners still see it as 'the dough area' and nothing else.

A few years ago those of us in early years education got the directive that not only was 'junk modelling' now going to be called 'recycled materials modelling' but 'the dough area' was going to undergo a name change too. It would now be referred to by the very grand title of 'the malleable materials' area. Many people gave an audible groan, thought it was to do with jumping on the latest terminology band wagon, and went off to laminate some more labels! But for me it made perfect sense, especially in relation to children's gross and fine motor dexterity.

I have already talked about the fact that children need to develop balance, hand-eye coordination, proprioception, upper body pivots, hand arches, finger pivots, grip and so on. All of these skills can be developed in the malleable materials area but they couldn't be in the dough area: the reason is that dough is not diverse enough.

As a substance dough is great and children can do a great deal with it. You can make it in a variety of colours, smells and textures which can be really effective if you are focussing on a sensory exploration or experience. When it comes to dexterity dough offers its best challenge to the mid range of development, especially if there is no adult engaged with the learning experience.

However to get really effective motor dexterity impact from our malleable materials area we need to think about how we stock it with a wide range of malleable materials, only one of which will be dough. Let's take some of the fundamental developments that we have talked about and see how we could translate them into an effective malleable materials area.

Gross motor upper body development

Focus

- balance
- hand-eye coordination
- bi-lateral movement
- crossing midline
- proprioception
- shoulder pivot

If we are trying to develop all of these skills with our children then they are not going to happen if we have simply created a space with table and chairs, some dough, rolling pins, dough cutting utensils and cup cake cases. We need a space that will require the children in it to use their sense of balance. They will need a space that is big enough to allow them to stretch and reach to their full capacity. We will need to provide a malleable material that promotes large movements and also encourages them to stretch using hand-eye coordination, proprioception and balance.

Points for action

Get rid of the chairs: Children don't need to sit down when they are using malleable materials. Standing will develop balance, proprioception, bi-lateral movement, cross midline development and shoulder pivot.

Give them space: Children at the earliest stages of development will need enough space to stretch their arms both to the front and to the side. Think of them as swimmers doing the breast stroke.

Provide a material that moves: If children need to develop that 'swimming' action then dough is not going to be the material for them as it doesn't 'move' enough. Ideally you would provide a material that is fluid enough to encourage the development of the pivots while also being solid enough to allow the children to squeeze it, to develop their palm arches and pincer movement. Something like couscous is good for this and it also won't hurt them if they eat it (be aware of any food allergies)! There are many more examples of possible malleable materials in Chapter 8, page 52.

Dress it for interest: So, you have identified your children's stage of development and you have created an appropriately sized space and given them an effective malleable material. Your only problem is getting them to go in it in the first place! That is where you 'dressing' the activity comes in. If you have a group of children who are interested in Ben 10 then link your chosen material with this theme! Make the couscous green and black, perhaps put some alien stickers under it that they have to clear the couscous to find. Throw in some plastic spiders and some large tweezers for good measure and challenge them on a talking peg to catch ten spiders. If it is going to be effective it has to be relevant but more than anything else it has to be engaging!

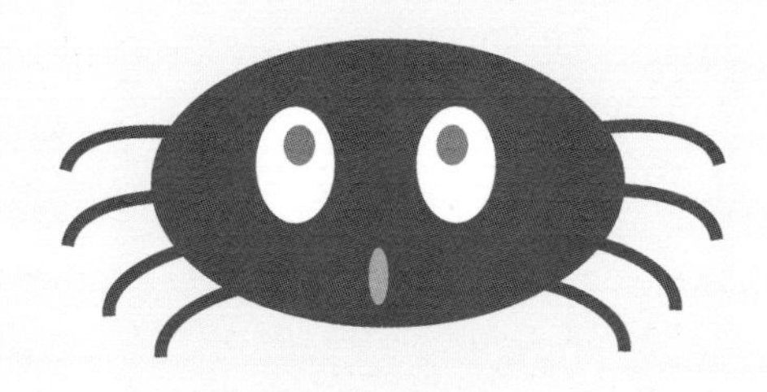

Gross motor mid body development

Focus

- balance
- hand-eye coordination
- bi-lateral movement
- crossing midline
- proprioception
- elbow pivot
- wrist pivot,
- palm arches
- pincer grip

Children at this stage are in the process of developing mid range dexterity skills and it is with this group that the use of dough and other substances of a similar texture and resistance come into their own. You can indeed change the colour, texture and smell of your dough but remember that doing that doesn't significantly change its malleability: it is still dough. A dough with a live ingredient like yeast will make it more stretchy and an oily dough will be more slippery so you can get some diversity within the range of flexibility.

Points for action

Get rid of the chairs: I still would not provide chairs as these children will not suffer for the lack of them. Plus experience tells me that if there are chairs available for some children and not others, the ones you don't want to sit down will take a chair and sit down anyway!

Give them appropriate space: Although these children's movements are not likely to be as gross as at the first stage of development they will still need enough space to bend their elbows and manipulate their malleable materials.

Provide material with stretch and resistance: It is all about the pull, push, squeeze and roll with these children. The material they work with has to require them to use their elbows and wrists to manipulate it as well as the palms of their hands and their finger joints.

Enhance with equipment: Add equipment such as cutters, rollers, moulds remembering to match them to skill development.

Dress for interest: Often it is the children with mid range dexterity who are the biggest group in your setting and therefore they can have the most diverse range of interests. What I tend to do is to go with the two most predominant interests of the group and dress the activity according to those. So you might have some brown dough which is very much themed and accessorised around an interest in dinosaurs and some pink sparkly dough which is accessorised around princesses. Regardless of gender, go with interest.

Fine motor development

Focus

- bi-lateral movement
- pincer grip
- finger pivots
- triangulation
- in-hand manipulation

This group of children are the ones who already show high levels of dexterity and are able to manipulate their mark making resources well. For them the focus in the malleable materials is all about high level resistance and small scale work focussing on their finger joints with particular attention on the final joint alongside in-hand manipulation.

Points for action

Still no chairs: This is not because balance, hand-eye coordination and proprioception are usually an issue for children with this level of development. It is purely because other children will sit on them if they are there. If all of your children were at this stage in their development then you might consider letting them have a sit down, although it will make no difference to the skill development they are focussing on.

Give them appropriate space: You really want these children to work on a small scale, so it often helps to give them the parameters of a small space to work in.

Provide materials that resist: Children at this stage in their development would benefit from working with materials like putty or stiff dough that require the fingers to work hard to manipulate. There are recipes for this type of malleable material in Chapter 8, page 52.

Enhance with equipment: Even though this area focuses on the use of a malleable material you can further enhance the skill development by introducing resources that require the children to use their finger joints to manipulate them.

Dress for interest: As with all of the resources that you put into this area, the children who need this level of manipulation need to be interested enough in how it is presented to want to come and have a go. Your assessment will have identified who the children are that need this level of challenge, all you need to do is to find out what they are interested in and dress your resources appropriately.

Of course, you only need to offer each level of provision if your assessment or observation identifies a need for it in your group. If you have no children who need to develop their real gross motor skills then you don't need to create an area for it. By the same token, if none of your children are showing great manual dexterity yet then don't create an area for that. As you will have realised, if you have children at all stages of development, then the one thing you are going to need is space. In that respect a table more often than not doesn't provide enough space for the provision to be effective so it is worth considering setting up a 'malleable materials bar' along a work surface. If the children are then facing a wall, put up some mirrors so that you can talk to them about what their arms, hands and fingers are doing and they can see for themselves.

There are daily programmes like Dough gym and Funky fingers (see Chapters 6 and 7) that will help you to make accurate and current assessment of your children's ability and provide a daily focussed challenge to move their learning forward.

When these areas are running as part of your continuous provision and there is not an adult working in them, you cannot guarantee that every child will go to exactly the right spot and access exactly the prescribed malleable material. But, what you have done is create the maximum potential for attainment and the minimum risk of failure. In addition any adult who is moving through the continuous provision will be very clear how the malleable materials area has been structured and if they see a child who is clearly engaged with a material which is not really appropriate for their stage of development they can either introduce a challenge or resource into their play or redirect them to the right one.

Chapter 4

Letter formation

This sort of activity can start as soon as children understand what shapes look like and what they are called. You can work with the children in short sharp bursts and make your activities as interactive and fun as possible. When I am doing this sort of thing I try and work with the children in small groups rather than a whole class. The reason for this is that not all children are at the same level of development in terms of their knowledge of shape and their gross motor dexterity. Also if I am working with a small group I can have some really focussed intervention that is going to have some impact on their development rather than just 'going through the motions'!

Getting started

A good place to start is to think about all of the patterns that children will eventually use in their handwriting – most of which are related to 2D shapes that they will be beginning to recognise.

Take each of the patterns in turn and using gross motor movements (think about your pivots) coach the children through how they form that shape either in the air or by making marks.

When children learn to write letters, and they really have to think about where they put their pencil and then which direction to move it in first, they have an internal dialogue with themselves. They need to talk the process through. What we want for children is that when they come to want to record letter shapes that they don't have to stop and think about what goes where because they have already rehearsed that internal dialogue over and over again.

When we are teaching any sort of early orientation work, talk is by far the best place to start. It is more effective than facing a group of children, trying to demonstrate how to draw a shape or letter in mid air, having to reverse the shape that we make so that it looks the right way round to them and then having to try and watch them all to see if they are going the right way or not!

Instead, start with getting everyone to talk it through. Before their finger hits the air or the waterlogged paintbrush hits the wall you need to talk, chant or sing it. In my experience, this sort of activity always works significantly better when it is done to music. Having said that, there needs to be some method in what you are doing. As much fun as it is to jump around with a scarf in each hand waving them about like a demented scarecrow, the children (and you) need to understand why they are doing it and not just what you want them to do.

A common situation that arises with emergent writers is one where the child has made a valiant effort to write something in what we would recognise as print (usually their name). Although they can tell us some of the letter sounds that they have used they have formed them in a most unique and peculiar way. As a practitioner you are faced with a dilemma. You know that self esteem is the biggest motivator for learning and that lack of it is the biggest inhibitor of learning. Yet, you also know that if this child continues to orientate their letter shapes in this way then this will become 'normal' to them and it will become almost impossible to get them out of the habit. So, should you correct them and explain they need to learn the proper letter formation or do you praise them so they walk away from you proudly clutching their 'writing'? Of course it has to be the second scenario – but in the pit of your stomach you know the day is going to have to come when you or someone else says 'Actually, you are doing it all wrong! Let me show you how to do it properly!'

My secret weapon in the fight against destroying self esteem is to get rid of the term 'properly' or 'the right way' and any others that are remotely similar. Instead I always go for 'different' which is useful because you are not saying 'I am right and you are wrong', you are just saying 'Let's try this another way'.

Forming letters

When a child is beginning to form recognisable letters and linking those letter sounds to shapes, they are entering a crucial phase. Not only in their phonic development, but also in laying the ground rules for how those shapes are best formed and how their pencil is best held to give them a style of writing that will aid speed, comfort and flexibility as their writing develops.

The key is to start early and start with talk. You need to pattern the language of writing in their head, so that whenever they go to pick up a pencil or form a letter in the early stages of development, they hear your voice chanting your mantras for handwriting. As a basic skill, handwriting can be fundamentally dull to start off with. If you then get your children involved in chanting dull and meaningless phrases on mass then you are likely to do more harm than good.

For real success and impact, letter formation work should not be done as a large group, but instead in a number of small groups. Group children by the shape or sound that they need to focus on and, if you are able, by a common interest. It is this interest that we are going to use to dress our handwriting activities in an effort to hide the possible mind numbing dullness!

Like many other features of effective teaching there are two stages to talking children out of their bad habits: the first is the introduction of the 'different' way, the second is the consolidation of the new skills that have been taught. This second stage is by far the hardest and is heavily reliant on spoken reminders and 'talk' cues. This method of teaching and correcting handwriting came about by complete accident (as many of the great ideas in my teaching career do) and was born out of one small boy's fascination with Star Wars.

This particular boy was thrilling us all with his desire to write. His phonic knowledge was coming on a treat and he was keen to record (little and often). The problem was that he was still using a palmer supinate grasp and pivoting from the elbow, his range of fine motor movement was not great and his letter orientation was all over the place. No letter started in the same place twice, sometimes he started at the bottom, sometimes the top and 'sticks' and 'tails' were added very precisely to letters that needed them but always as a completely separate entity and invariably not in the right place.

Writing opportunities

In an effort to support this child's development and that of other children who were at a similar stage, I decided that I would get all of the children to sign in when they arrived each morning. This was something that I had done many times before and knew that it was a technique that existed as part of what I perceived to be 'accepted good practice'.

What I had never done was to actually analyse the effectiveness and impact of signing in as an aid to mark making development. As I was struggling to be effective in my strategies to support this boy in his mark making so far, I was watching how he would respond to this routine. What I observed over the next couple of weeks really challenged my view of the use of signing in in this way and I have never done it since.

The main principal behind getting the children to sign in was to give them another opportunity to practise writing their names. I also felt that it was good for their self esteem as they had a chance to make their own personal mark to show everyone that they had arrived every day. What I found was that some children loved signing in, but unfortunately these didn't turn out to be the children that I was targeting. These were the children who could already write (often girls) who you would find whipping out a calligraphy pen from their book bag and producing an accurate replica of some eighteenth century illuminated script before skipping to the carpet!

When I say that they could write, they could in the sense that they could produce shapes that corresponded to letter sounds. Often these shapes looked very neat. On closer inspection of the children actually in the process of writing I was amazed at the range of grips there were on show, not to mention the styles of letter formation that did the job for now but would invariably impact on their progress later on.

By giving these children lots of opportunities for unsupported writing, I was actually consolidating their bad habits rather than instilling good ones. I am of course not saying that a child in their early stages of development should not write unless accompanied by an adult. But as practitioners we should consider carefully what balance of opportunities we make available to children for mark making and how those opportunities impact on their development.

One of the other things I noticed about signing in was that children watched each other write. At first I thought this was a good thing as some children might be inspired by the writing of others. It is true that this can sometimes be the case, but in my experience the signing in table just serves to lower self esteem of the children whose skills are more emergent, especially the boys. This was often compounded by the language of adults in relation to children's efforts, 'That is beautiful Charlotte' as opposed to 'Great try Connor, I will come and help you in an minute'. Both statements sound positive, except the second, although dressed in positive language (and intentions) is actually very negative and a real self esteem killer.

As a result of my signing in observations I focussed far more on planning for an effective balance between opportunities to independently mark make alongside effective adult intervention for letter formation and orientation. I also wanted to have verbal 'cues' that I could use to remind children about their handwriting that were effective, positive and that I could just 'drop' into their play without having to railroad it with a deadly handwriting session.

What had become really clear to me was that it was not the physical aspect of forming letters in handwriting practice that was really having an impact on their improvement, it was the verbal mantras that we were using when we were describing to them how to form each letter. Even when their grip was still very emergent and nowhere near triangulating they could still start in the right place and then head in the right direction, just on a much bigger scale.

I discovered very quickly that if you can get children to learn the letter formation mantras as they are beginning to link sounds to letter shapes and attempting to record them then when they come to record, however gross motor their movements, the orientation and formation are correct.

Chapter 5

Writing like a Jedi

The first school that I taught in favoured the use of 'underwriting' in reception. This is a process where the adult writes out a word or sentence and then leaves the child to 'copy' that sentence underneath. It sounds quite plausible in theory (especially when you don't know any better), but in truth it serves little purpose other than to reinforce bad habits and further confuse and frustrate confused children.

Although a fairly constant feature in my children's books, 'Monday morning news' was the time we were specifically asked to use underwriting. There would be five groups of children to get round before playtime and they all needed a sentence and a picture about their weekend to be recorded in their book. The whole session ended up like some Olympic time trial where I galloped around tables with a coloured felt tip in hand (it looked nice in their books on parents' evening) asking children what they did at the weekend and then writing it down.

Once I had manipulated some sort of coherent sentence out of them and written it down in my colourful felt tip, I was off to the next one while my previous victim was left to 'have a go' at copying letters that they were not familiar with and that they hadn't got the phonic knowledge to read.

If they forgot what they had said (probably because they made it up in the first place) then you would get some interesting sentence and picture matches. I remember one little girl who said she had been swimming with her granny and then drew a picture of Shrek. I never met her granny in the flesh but I am sure whatever she looked like, Shrek was a bit of a harsh comparison! The little girl just couldn't remember what she had said and had no way of finding out. My conclusion was that underwriting doesn't work! Instead, it is far better to encourage children to use their emergent mark making skills and then assess what they can do for attainment and next steps.

Why 'write like a Jedi'?

I came up with this technique as a 'boy heavy' reception class teacher in the early 1990's when Star Wars was 'big news' in my class. The key to any successful learning is of course engagement so make sure however you choose to 'dress' your handwriting practice has them jumping up and down with excitement and not hiding under the water tray.

Writing like a Jedi has since morphed into a myriad of other inspirations for writing but the basic principles have always remained the same. It is:

- talk and gross motor movement based
- designed to target small groups of children for specific development
- regular
- short
- rooted in children's interests
- fun!

After being away on a day's training I came back to school to be debriefed by my teaching assistant on the previous day's fun and excitement that I had missed. We were looking through some of the mark making that the children had produced and the topic of one particular boy and his orientation came up again. We were actually discussing if we thought some Star Wars themed handwriting sheets might help when the idea struck me.

When all the children were seated on the carpet I said that I wanted to tell them about the very exciting day I had had and the most amazing thing that I had learnt to do. If my memory serves me right the actual carpet session was delivered with great drama and suspense! I told them that I had been on a course where I had met none other than Luke Skywalker! (Okay, so I lied – but it is no worse than Father Christmas or the Tooth Fairy!) You could hear an audible intake of breath from the target audience. Not only had it been a huge thrill to meet Luke but we had gone on the course to learn how to write like a Jedi!

I took great pains to explain that this was different from the way that 'we' all wrote but that it was amazing because you got to do it with a light sabre! So, 'would anyone on the carpet like to learn how to write like a Jedi warrior?' Of course they would! Now I had high level engagement, I just had to make sure that what I was going to get the children to do was actually going to impact on their ability to mark make and not just going to be 'all show and no substance' which can be the curse of an early years activity.

The initiative starts with patterning of language, coupled with a gross motor movement. Even if the children are actually using wrist or finger pivot, it is easy for them to translate the action to where they are currently working whereas it is much harder to go in the opposite direction. I usually work with a small group of children, no more than six, and we focus on a particular letter or group of letters that shared a similar shape or orientation. So what is it that 'teaches' children how to form letters correctly? It is not their ability to triangulate or how clearly the example has been produced, it is the language that is used and repeated for the formation of each one.

Things you will need

Whatever the 'theme' of the session or the particular interests of the group, you will need a box of props that the children are going to use to help them to make the movements. For writing like a Jedi you will need good light sabres, not the ones that might be in your outdoor continuous provision. For this activity they need to have the 'desire' factor so it is worth paying a bit extra for those that light up or make a bit of noise. These 'special' light sabres should be saved for this activity to maintain what I would call their 'wantability'.

If you haven't got the budget for a flashing light sabre and you are feeling creative then you can always make your own. This is not as complex as it sounds and you only need three things: a pool noodle, some silver duct tape and some black insulating tape. Pool noodles are great for this because they are light, which makes them easier for the children to manipulate. Also, if they happen to whack each other (by accident of course) it doesn't hurt as much!

Simply cut the pool noodles into manageable lengths, based on the height and coordination skills of the children who is going to be using them. For smaller children use a shorter length of pool noodle as they will find this much easier to manipulate and orientate.

One important thing to remember is that waving around a pool noodle or any other sort of light sabre is not going to improve the children's handwriting, although it may help with their balance if you are lucky.

The key to this strategy working is talk. The assumption that you can only write what you can talk doesn't just apply to structuring sentences and using imaginative language: it also applies to the process of handwriting.

If a child was very physically dexterous and could triangulate their pencil beautifully and you showed them a 'g' and asked them to reproduce it without any previous experience or further instruction, the chances are their orientation and letter formation would still be incorrect.

Getting started

First I get the children to stand up. Apart from the fact that it is difficult to use a light sabre when you are sitting down, standing gives children more space for a greater range of movement. Part of the process of becoming a writer is the development of balance and proprioception (your ability to manage the space that you are in). Standing up rather than sitting down helps children to develop their sense of balance, proprioception as well as hand-eye coordination and depth perception – not to mention a bit of gross motor muscle toning!

I would often position the children in a line for this sort of activity so that you can stand behind them and help them to move their arms correctly if they are struggling. Start your session with a talk through: no actions, just talk. Where does this shape/letter start? Then where do we go? You want them to be really clear about what it is that is about to happen. It can be done indoors or out, wherever the children are going to engage most.

Next I would do a demonstration with my light sabre, talking about all of the 'essentials' for effective writing like a Jedi: straight back, legs shoulder width apart, big strong movements, no wobbling!

You can either get the children to create the letter shapes from memory, or for extra support project or draw the letter onto the wall or whiteboard and get them to 'virtually' trace it in the air. You might want to give the children the opportunity to do a dry run with an 'imaginary' light sabre to check that they have got the language and the appropriate movement first.

Now they can get their hands on a light sabre. Even though there are strict codes of conduct for becoming a Jedi writer, light sabres are very exciting for some children so expect a bit of giddiness and enjoy the fact that they are so engaged in a handwriting activity!

When the children have their light sabres you are all going to work together. It is important to remind the children that they have to state the name of the letter or shape and then talk it out constantly as they are making it.

The last, but equally important part of this initiative is the use of music. In all of my experience of using this method with hundreds of children, the music makes a significant difference. The rhythm helps them with their dialogue about what they are doing and they just enjoy the sheer fun of it. Write like a Jedi to a disco version of the Star Wars theme. It never fails!

Making it work

As with any teaching strategy, the more you put into it, the more you get out of it. If you just give your children a few cheap light sabres and some letters on a whiteboard and say 'have a go at that' you are likely to get limited results. If you link your teaching to children's interests and make your activities fun and aspirational, then you are likely to get some brilliant results.

Although my write like a Jedi technique was initially inspired by a boy, I need to make it clear that when you plan any sort of initiative you are planning for interest not gender. Of course it will happen that there will be some areas of interest that are predominantly favoured by either girls or boys, but we should never be planning for 'girls' and 'boys' we should always just be planning for 'children'.

Writing like a Jedi morphed into Sparkle writing (with a wand), Princess writing, Buzz Lightyear laser challenge (with a Buzz Lightyear glove made from a sports sock, a laser pen and some green insulating tape), Pirate writing (done with your cutlass), Fairy writing (done with artificial flowers and chiffon scarves) to name but a few!

When children do then come to do their mark making either with an adult or independently then you can remind them, rather than to do it 'properly' to remember to do their Princess writing, Buzz Lightyear writing and so on. If you are focusing on a particular letter that a child is not forming correctly then you can remind them to do their 'princess 'e''.

Dressing the activity for interest gives you the mental 'jogger' that you need to instantly remind children about what your expectation is but in a way that makes them think 'happy thoughts' rather than misery over tracing paper torture! It has to be engaging, it has to make sense to the child and be done regularly if you want to have impact. I guarantee you, if you do it, you will get great results.

In essence, everything I have described here could be considered a form of rote learning: repeating an instruction again and again until it sticks and recall becomes automatic. The brain's natural function is to try and make sense of what we experience, it will look for patterns and relationships in the information that it takes in and then make links between past and present experiences. The more meaningful or engaging the learning the better chance it has of sticking. In that respect, rote teaching can be very dull and disjointed from children's understanding and thus slows down the learning process and significantly limits the levels of engagement and understanding.

In terms of teaching through talk, rote learning is often criticised as being meaningless and disconnected from children's understanding. In this case I would argue that the learning is very much linked to children's interests and understanding. There is repetition that is helping the language of the learning to become familiar but the combination of language, physical movement, music and high level of interest and engagement is what makes the learning powerful.

The key to its success, as always, is engagement. If you sat at a table with a skinny lined writing book and a sharpened pencil and drilled children in their letter formation learning through rote, they would probably disengage very quickly. The fact that you have 'dressed' the teaching in an area that interests them and you are delivering it in a physical manner will give you high levels of engagement which in turn will produce high levels of attainment.

Chapter 6

Dough Gym

The basic concept behind 'Dough Gym' comes from the same philosophy as writing like a Jedi. It is about turning something that is often perceived by children as a negative feeling about their own abilities into a positive. Making a 'can't do' into a 'can do'. I used the first version of it when I was a classroom teacher in the early 1990's and although it has evolved as my knowledge of physical development has grown, the principles have stayed pretty much the same.

It all started with a group of boys who had no interest in mark making whatsoever. Because they were not making progress and showed no interest they were 'banished' to the table at the back of the room every morning to 'practise'. They hated every minute of it, made frequent trips to the toilet throughout the session and made no quantifiable progress with their mark making. The reason for this was because they were not yet physically ready to be successful in the tasks that I was giving to them but more importantly they were completely disengaged and uninterested.

Rather than enabling them to become successful mark makers and writers I was confirming to them that when they were asked to 'come and sit at red table' or 'come and do a special job' that they were about to suffer death by boredom. Worst of all, by trying to help them make progress I was actually undermining their self confidence. Every morning was started for them by engaging in a task that they hated and couldn't do. Who would want to start their day like that?

The solution was to marry appropriate provision and activities with some high level engagement. Thus 'Dough Gym' was born.

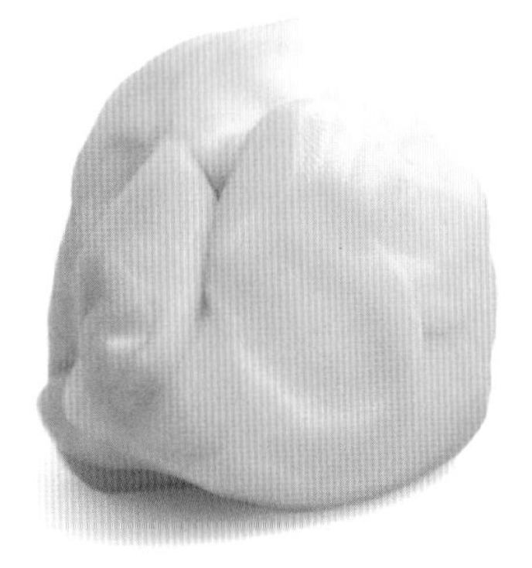

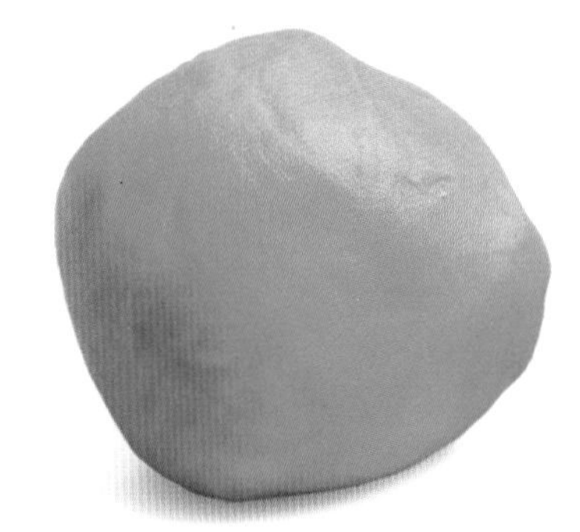

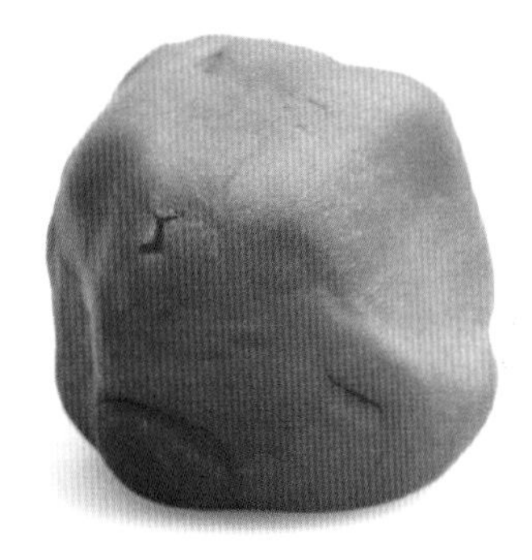

What is Dough Gym?

- **Dough Gym is a gym for children where you work out with dough** – simple!
- **Dough Gym is a specific daily intervention** – to have impact it has to be regular and consistent.
- **Dough Gym is exclusive** – you need to make the children who need this intervention feel special and chosen for all of the right reasons, not just because they are failing. I usually work with a maximum of eight children, not a whole group.
- **Dough Gym is planned** – this initiative is about targeting specific areas of development. It won't work if you just slap a bit of dough around!
- **Dough Gym is done to music** – I have found that this is key to its success. Children are highly engaged by music and the beat is crucial when it comes to performing the Dough Gym moves. Choose your music carefully. Something that is popular and current is far more likely to get high levels of engagement than working out to 'Jesus' hands were kind hands'!

Things you will need

1. **Space:** If you are working with up to eight children who are going to be practising a series of gross motor movements then make sure you have enough space to stop them from knocking each other out!
2. **Membership cards:** Every Gym member needs a membership card that they can keep in their drawer and show to the Dough Gym leader (you!) every time they work out.
3. **Certificate:** Dough Gym is an intervention. Children wouldn't stay on it indefinitely so I always gave them a certificate when they had completed their turn (often this was around a half term).
4. **Labelling/posters:** As this is a Dough Gym it is important to brand it as such with lots of fitness labels posters and information. It is good to have a mix between commercially produced and child created versions.
5. **Dough:** This might seem like a bit of an obvious one, but every child needs to have a very large piece of dough to work with. As a general rule of thumb, they need a piece of dough as big as their head! If you make it in a pan, it is about a pan full each.
6. **Music:** Something current that the children will know that has got a good steady beat to it. Your Dough Gym session will last the length of the piece of music. Around three to four minutes is about enough.
7. **Workout routine:** Dough Gym has a series of moves each that supports a different area of development from shoulder pivot to pincer grip. Over time the children become very familiar with the names of each move and are able to change them on command. Nevertheless your workout routine should match the needs of the children in the session.

How does a session work?

Dough Gym needs to take place at the beginning or end of a session so that you are not pulling children out of continuous provision or away from areas of interest and exploration. I always prefer to do mine at the beginning of the day. As you want Dough Gym to carry a bit of prestige and have the 'enviability factor' it is better if it is done in your main space and that children aren't taken off to another room to do it! You can run Dough Gym and Funky Fingers (see Chapter 7) at the same time so that all children are having a daily intervention that is supporting and extending their gross and fine motor development.

To start the Dough Gym children present you with their membership cards and then take up their places. It is important that the children stand, as part of this initiative is to develop their balance, posture, proprioception, hand-eye coordination and bilateral movement which is less effective when you sit down.

Children's backs need to be straight and their legs shoulder width apart. They will find it very tempting to bend forward thus using their back rather than their shoulders and arms to support the dough. I always tell mine to squeeze their bottoms as this tightens the 'core' and helps prevent bending.

When the music starts, begin with shoulder pivots and arm stretches utilising the biggest range of movement interspersed with wrist, hand and finger exercises. Use the dough for resistance work: anything from squashing it with a flat palm and a straight arm to pinching small bits out of it. The large ball of dough is also useful for developing arm muscles and pivots by lifting as well as hand arches and finger pivots by squeezing.

The session should be fast paced and hard work but most of all fun. You want to keep the children coming back for more. The role of the Dough Gym leader is quite like that of a slightly crazed aerobics instructor. Once the children become familiar with a few basic moves then you will be able to sequence them just by calling out the name of the move when you want the children to change. As the children become more proficient, you can add more moves and create a more complex and challenging work out.

Dough Gym moves

Around the world

Around the world: *Children hold their complete piece of dough with both hands. With arms outstretched and with no bend in their elbows they take their dough in a complete circle as if it was a moon going around the Earth.*

Milk the cow

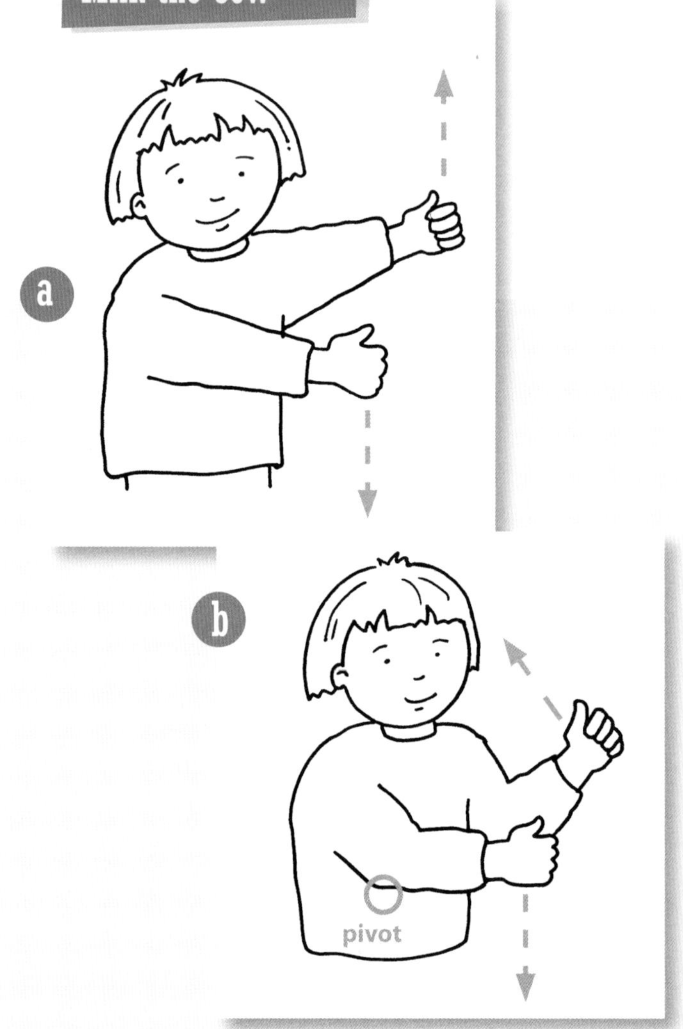

Milk the cow: *(a) This can be done with completely straight arms or by bending at the elbow. With straight arms the children stretch their arms out in front of them and make a fist. They move their arms up and down alternately squeezing their fists as they do so.*
(b) *For elbow pivot, the children start in the same position, but instead of using the shoulder pivot they bend alternately from the elbow, squeezing their fist on the way down.*

Sharks

Sharks: *This is a palm arches and finger manipulation exercise. The children bend their elbows with both palms facing their stomachs, fingers tight together: this is the shark's tail. The children push their thumbs straight up in the air. Keeping their fingers tightly together on each hand and their thumbs straight. The children have to bend and straighten their knuckles to make their sharks 'swim'.*

Jazz hands

Jazz hands: *The children start with their arms by their side with an outstretched palm and slowly raise their arm while keeping the palm spread. When their arm is fully extended they bring it back down again. For the development of an elbow pivot, the arm begins down by their side, but instead of the whole arm being kept straight the child bends their elbow keeping the top of the arm next to the body.*

Lasso

pivot

Lasso: *Children start with their arms out to the side at shoulder height (like a scarecrow) and then bend at the elbow. They then make a fist, as if they are holding a lasso. While maintaining the bend in the elbow and a fist, they rotate their wrists either alternately or at the same time ending with a complete arm extension out in front of them as if they are throwing the lasso.*

Swim

Swim: *The children begin with their elbows bent, palms down, thumbs touching each other and the backs of their hands under their chin. Keeping their thumbs together they push their hands out in front of them until their arms are fully extended, before bringing their hand back under their chin to start again (like breast stroke).*

There are lots more Dough Gym moves and routines at **www.abcdoes.com.**

Chapter 7

Funky Fingers

Dough Gym is a very effective programme for children who really need to work on their upper body and gross motor development, but there may well be children in our settings who need more focussed input on their hands, fingers and grip.

Although you can add resources to the dough to support this development the intervention will not be as specific. When I was delivering the Dough Gym programme with my designated group I sometimes found that they became a bit self conscious. All the other children would stand and watch as we flung our dough around to loud music! The other children were also constantly asking for a go and starting to emulate Dough Gym in their own free play.

Initially I decided that every now and then I would give each child in the class a small piece of dough and we would all do a very abridged version of the Dough Gym programme at the same time. This was indeed great fun, but in terms of attainment and impact it wasn't particularly useful.

What is Funky Fingers?

What I needed was activities for the other children to do while Dough Gym was taking place. That way no one would be standing and staring and our Dough Gym music wouldn't be bothering anyone else because we would all be working out to it. That is when Funky Fingers was born.

As I have previously said, there is no point in just getting children to squash a few bits of dough in time to music if it's not going to have any impact on their fine motor development. So the first port of call is assessment: you need to know where the children are currently, in terms of their dexterity and then identify what the next steps are.

To do this assessment you need to take into account a child's grip with a variety of objects of different sizes and also their ability to use their own fingers, or manipulate apparatus or resources to pick up small objects. Then you can use this information to create activities that will challenge and extend the children.

When it comes to Funky Fingers activities, the speed at which you ask the children to perform the activity or the number of times you ask them to complete the task in a given time frame can really increase the level of challenge.

Sometimes you will get a group of children whose dexterity is amazing, they could pick up a speck of dust with one eye closed! For these children I usually organise some sort of activity that you can do to music which is linked to the principles of brain gym. One setting I have worked with does a very effective brain gym Zumba with lots of cross body, bi-lateral movements and a couple of maracas thrown in for good measure!

How does a session work?

One group of children will be working with an adult having a Dough Gym session. The rest of the children will be split into groups identified by your assessment of their need and stage of development. With two adults it is advisable to have no more than five groups in total (including Dough Gym).

For example:

Group 1 – Dough Gym

Group 2 – Pompoms and tweezers

Group 3 – Threading on skewers

Group 4 – Spiders in jelly

Group 5 – Zumba

An adult would need to be stationed with the Dough Gym and the Zumba children as they need direct input and will be following constant instruction. The other groups have a task to complete:

Group 2: How many pompoms can you move from the pot to the egg box with the tweezers?

Group 3: How fast can you fill the skewer with beads and then empty it again?

I tend to do my Dough Gym and Funky Fingers at the same time every day, usually after the children have had a 'sitting' time, like carpet time or a direct teaching session. Everyone should know where their Funky Fingers group is and on your command they should take their places! Put the music on and everyone is working at the same time. You will be amazed how tiring working with dough and pompoms can be!

The Funky Fingers activities stay for a week and they are only used at 'Funky Fingers time' and not as part of continuous provision. This helps you to ensure that you can really monitor how the children are using the activities to make sure they have maximum impact, it also stops the children from getting bored with them.

The easiest way I have found for managing your Funky Fingers time is to have your activities in a box or on a tray under the table each morning. While one adult is finishing the carpet session then another can easily lift the resources out onto the table tops, or you can get the children to do it at the beginning of the session. Once the session is over the boxes can go back under the table out of the way.

Your Funky Fingers and Dough Gym session does not have to take place exclusively inside. You could take a group out into your outdoor area during this time to engage in some upper body physical tasks, although for practical reasons, they might have to do without the music. You could always sing!

The important thing is that you match the provision to the needs of the children. If you have a large group that you think would benefit from some Dough Gym input then you could create two Dough Gym groups, each led by a different adult. The other children would be completing Funky Fingers activities during this time.

As the children become more proficient in their skills then you should increase the dexterity challenge of the activities that you offer them. Make sure that you record this progress to show evidence of how your environment, planning and intervention is having a direct impact on attainment.

Funky Fingers activities

Dough balloons

What you need

- Party balloons
- Play dough
- Plastic bottle

What to do

1. Mix a batch of play dough.
2. Cut the top third off a plastic bottle (to make a funnel).
3. Stretch the end of the balloon over the neck of the bottle.
4. Roll one cup of the dough into a sausage.
5. Feed the dough sausage through the bottle neck and into the balloon.
6. Tie the balloon.

Activity

Children can squeeze the balloons in colour sequence or against the clock. To make the activity more difficult put the balloons in a tray with baby oil to make them extra slippery!

Areas of development

• hand-eye coordination • bi-lateral movement • elbow pivot • wrist pivot • palm arches • pincer grip • knuckle pivot • PIP joint • DIP joint.

Finger knitting – one finger

What you need

- Thick wool

What to do

1. Take your flat palm and point it towards the ceiling.
2. Take the wool and trap the end of it between your thumb and forefinger.
3. Bend down your second, third and fourth fingers (so it looks like you are pointing).
4. Wrap the wool around the middle of your finger twice.
5. Take the back loop of wool pull it over the top of the front loop and off the end of your finger.
6. Take your wool and wrap it around the middle of your finger in front of the existing loop and then repeat the process.

Activity

Children can use the long knitted strings that they create for anything from Spider Man's web to coiling into a flower. The possibilities are endless.

Areas of development

• hand-eye coordination • bi-lateral movement • wrist pivot • palm arches • pincer grip • knuckle pivot • PIP joint • DIP joint.

Painting with elastic bands

What you need

- Elastic bands
- Pencil
- Paint
- Paper

What to do

1. Wrap an elastic band several times around the end of a pencil until it is tight.
2. Take five or six other elastic bands and attach them to the end of the pencil by lifting the tight band and slipping the end of the loose band underneath to make a type of paintbrush.

Activity

Dip the 'loose' elastic bands into paint and make a pattern by twirling the pencil between your fingers.

Areas of development

• hand-eye coordination • elbow pivot • wrist pivot • palm arches • pincer grip • knuckle pivot • PIP joint • DIP joint.

Glue and string balls

What you need

- PVA glue
- String or wool
- Balloons
- Egg cup or small yogurt pot

What to do

1. Mix PVA glue with a little bit of water until it is the consistency of double cream.
2. Cut the wool or string into lengths and soak in the PVA and water.
3. Blow a little bit of air into the balloons so that it makes a small ball shape.
4. Place your balloon (knot down) in your egg cup or yogurt pot.

Activity

Standing up, the children take pieces of glue-soaked string and lay them over and wrap them around the balloons until they have created a 'cage' effect. Leave to dry overnight. Burst the balloon and they will have created small string and glue balls.

Areas of development

• balance • hand-eye coordination • bi-lateral movement • shoulder pivot • elbow pivot • wrist pivot • palm arches • pincer grip • knuckle pivot • PIP joint.

Paper plane

What you need

- A4 paper
- Hole punch
- Two elastic bands
- Pencil

What to do

1. Fold the paper to make a plane.
2. Punch a hole in the bottom of the plane about 3 cm from the front.
3. Loop one elastic band through the hole. Feed it through itself and pull to create a knot.
4. Loop the other band repeatedly around the end of a pencil until it can be looped no further to create a collar.

Activity

Take the elastic band from the bottom of the plane and loop it over the collar at the end of the pencil. Hold the pencil tight with a fist and pull back the plane with a strong pincer grip. Whenever you are ready…fire!

Areas of development

• balance • hand-eye coordination • bi-lateral movement • proprioception • shoulder pivot • elbow pivot • palm arches • pincer grip • knuckle pivot • PIP joint • DIP joint.

Pegs on a box

What you need

- A box (vary the size for amount of challenge needed)
- Clothes pegs
- Timer

What to do

1. Put the pegs in a pile on one side of the child and the empty box on the other.

Activity

Standing up, the children have to see how many pegs they can pick up with one hand (one at a time) and then peg them to the side of the empty box. If they get really quick at this, their challenge is to unpeg them and put them back.

Areas of development

• hand-eye coordination • bi-lateral movement • crossing midline • proprioception • shoulder pivot • elbow pivot • wrist pivot • palm arches • pincer grip • knuckle pivot.

Milk carton catcher

What you need

- Plastic milk carton
- Scissors
- Pompoms or small balls

What to do

1. Cut out a section of the milk carton leaving the handle intact (see photograph). Tape any sharp edges.
2. Use large cartons for an easier challenge.

Activity

Children either have one pom pom ball attached to their 'carton catcher' which they throw up and then catch on their own or another child or adult throws them pompoms or balls for them to catch.

Areas of development

• balance • hand-eye coordination • bi-lateral movement • crossing midline • proprioception • shoulder pivot • elbow pivot • wrist pivot • palm arches • knuckle pivot.

Paper cup poppers

What you need

- Paper or plastic cups
- Balloons
- Pompoms or mini marshmallows

What to do

1. Cut the top third off a deflated balloon.
2. Take the bottom two thirds of the balloon and stretch it over the bottom of a paper cup leaving the part that you would blow into hanging down.
3. Put a pompom into the bottom of the cup.

Activity

Holding the cup with one hand pull down the mouthpiece of the balloon using a pincer grip with the other and release. The pompom will jump out of the balloon. Now try and catch it.

Areas of development

• balance • hand-eye coordination • bi-lateral movement • crossing midline • proprioception • elbow pivot • wrist pivot • palm arches • pincer grip.

Paperclip in water

What you need

- Plastic storage jar
- Paperclips
- Water magnets

What to do

1. Fill the jar with water.
2. Drop the paperclips into the jar.
3. Put the lid on.

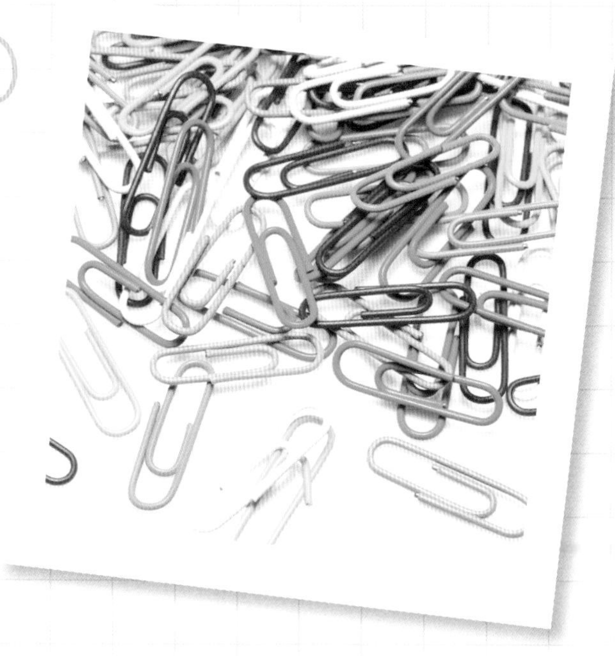

Activity

Use the water magnets to try and lift the paperclips from the bottom to the top of the jar. Challenge the children to catch more than one, have a paperclip race or beat the clock.

Areas of development

• hand-eye coordination • shoulder pivot • elbow pivot • wrist pivot • palm arches • pincer grip.

Pipe cleaners in a jar

What you need

- Pipe cleaners
- Scissors
- Plastic storage jar
- Magnets

What to do

1. Cut the pipe cleaners into 2 cm lengths.
2. Put them into the storage jar.
3. Replace the lid.

Activity

Use the magnets to catch and lift the pipe cleaners, make patterns or race each other.

Areas of development

• hand-eye coordination • shoulder pivot • elbow pivot • wrist pivot • palm arches • pincer grip.

Paper in a picture frame

What you need

- Plastic picture frame with Perspex or plastic cover (not glass)
- Paper
- Whiteboard markers

What to do

1. Put paper into the picture frame behind the Perspex.
2. Use plain paper, wide lined or narrow lined depending on the ability of the children.

Activity

The children can use the frame as an alternative to a whiteboard, writing on it with a whiteboard marker. You can vary the size of frame and the thickness of the marker depending on the dexterity of the child.

Areas of development

• balance • hand-eye coordination • shoulder pivot • elbow pivot • wrist pivot • palm arches • pincer grip • knuckle pivot • PIP joint • DIP joint.

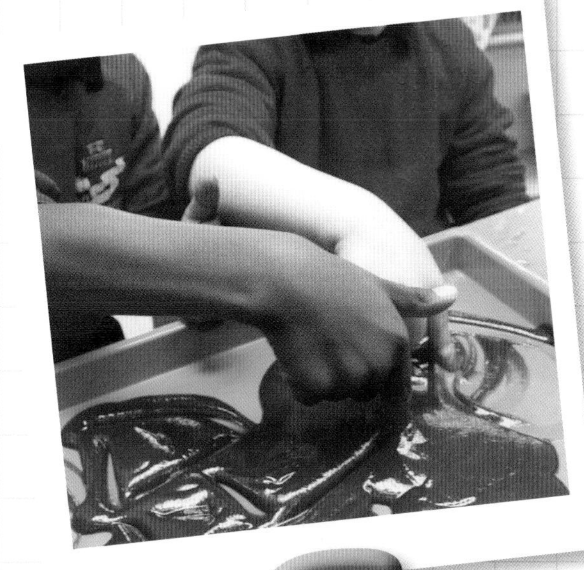

Writing in blood (tomato sauce!)

What you need

- Tomato sauce
- Builder's tray

What to do

1. Squirt the sauce into the tray.

Activity

Use hands, fingers or utensils to mark make or draw in the sauce. Vary the size of the tray and the size of the utensils depending on ability.

Areas of development

• hand-eye coordination • bi-lateral movement • crossing midline • shoulder pivot • elbow pivot • wrist pivot • palm arches • pincer grip • knuckle pivot • PIP joint • DIP joint (depending on size).

Paper plate hoopla

What you need

- Paper plates
- Paint
- Scissors
- Cardboard tube
- Dough

What to do

1. Cut out the middle of the paper plate to make a hoop.
2. Paint the remaining surrounds different colours.
3. Push the cardboard tube into the dough to make a post.

Activity

Children toss the paper plate hoops over the cardboard tube post. Increase the distance for more challenge.

Areas of development

• balance • hand-eye coordination • bi-lateral movement • crossing midline • proprioception • shoulder pivot • elbow pivot • wrist pivot • palm arches • pincer grip.

Buttons and button holes

What you need

- Lengths of ribbon
- Buttons
- Needle and thread
- Felt pieces
- Scissors

What to do

1. Stitch a button to the end of a piece of ribbon.
2. Cut slits the width of your button into the felt pieces.

Activity

The children have to push the button with the ribbon on the end through the felt button holes, collecting the pieces of felt on the ribbon. Vary the sizes of the button for challenge. Also introduce a timer for some 'speed buttoning'.

Areas of development

• hand-eye coordination • wrist pivot • palm arches • pincer grip • knuckle pivo • PIP joint • DIP joint.

Nuts and bolts

What you need

- Nuts
- Bolts
- Tray
- Timer

What to do

1. Unscrew the nuts from the bolts and mix them in the tray.

Activity

Children have to use both hands to find a nut and a bolt and screw them together. Once they have done them all, they can unscrew them again!

Areas of development

• hand-eye coordination • elbow pivot • wrist pivot • palm arches • pincer grip • knuckle pivot • PIP joint • DIP joint.

Golf tees and melon

What you need

- A melon
- Golf tees
- Hammer
- Builder's tray
- Small tubs

What to do

1. Cut the melon in half and lay it skin side up on a builder's tray.
2. Put the golf tees into a small tub so that they are tightly packed.

Activity

Children have to pick out a golf tee from the container and then hammer it into the half melon.

Areas of development

• hand-eye coordination • bi-lateral movement • proprioception • elbow pivot • wrist pivot • palm arches • pincer grip.

Threading skewers

What you need

- Dough
- Wooden skewers
- Penne pasta
- Beads
- Straws
- Scissors

What to do

1. Make a batch of dough and make into three balls.
2. Insert a skewer into each ball of dough.
3. Cut up the straw into 1 cm pieces.
4. Put the straw pieces, beads and pasta into a bowl.

Activity

Standing up, the children sort the contents of the bowl onto separate skewers. If they are quick they can take them all off again.

Areas of development

• balance • hand-eye coordination • bi-lateral movement • proprioception • shoulder pivot • elbow pivot • wrist pivot • palm arches • pincer grip • knuckle pivot.

Lentils, rice and peas

What you need

- Large bowl
- Dried lentils
- Uncooked rice
- Dried peas
- Tweezers
- Three small yogurt pots
- Timer

What to do

1. Mix all of the dry ingredients in a large bowl.

Activity

The children use the tweezers to pick the different ingredients out of the bowl and sort them into the yogurt pots before their time runs out. For extra challenge ask the children to use their fingers instead of tweezers.

Areas of development

• elbow pivot • wrist pivot • palm arche • pincer grip • knuckle pivot • PIP joint • DIP joint.

Football fingers

What you need

- Ping pong balls
- Finger football boots (or just fingers)
- Green paper
- Art straws
- Sticky tape
- Table top
- Paper (for keeping score)

What to do

1. Make a mini football pitch by using the green paper for grass and the straws for white lines.
2. Put the finger football boots onto your fingers.

Activity

Standing up, the children take turns to shoot the ping pong ball at the goal, recording their scores as they go.

Areas of development

• balance • hand-eye coordination • bi-lateral movement • crossing midline • proprioception • shoulder pivot • elbow pivot • wrist pivot • palm arches • knuckle pivot.

Marshmallows and bendy straws

What you need

- Pack of bendy straws
- Scissors
- Marshmallows
- Container
- Tweezers

What to do

1. Cut the straws into different lengths, some straight and some with bends.
2. Put the marshmallows into the container.

Activity

Children take a marshmallow with a pair of tweezers and the push it to the end of a straw. Keep repeating the process until the creation is complete (see photo above).

Areas of development

• hand-eye coordination • palm arches • pincer grip • knuckle pivot • PIP joint • DIP joint.

Pipe cleaner coil modelling

What you need

- Tall pot or tube
- Pipe cleaners
- Pencils of different widths
- Tweezers

What to do

1. Put the pipe cleaners into a tall pot or tube.

Activity

Children can take a pipe cleaner with their tweezers then make a coil by wrapping it around a pencil. Once they have made a number of coils they can model with them.

Areas of development

• hand-eye coordination • palm arches • pincer grip • knuckle pivot • PIP joint • DIP joint.

Shower stickers and beads

What you need

- Shower stickers
- Beads
- Tweezers
- Timer

What to do

1. Put the beads into a container.
2. Place the shower stickers onto a table with the sucker cups facing upwards.
3. Position the container with the beads an arm's length away from the shower sticker.

Activity

Standing up, the children reach forward, and using the tweezers take a bead and place it in one of the sucker cups of the shower sticker. They must try and fill all of the cups before the time runs out.

Areas of development

• hand-eye coordination • shoulder pivot • elbow pivo • wrist pivot • palm arche • pincer grip • knuckle pivot.

Matching pegs

What you need

- Paint colour charts (two of each chart)
- Clothes pegs
- Container
- Timer

What to do

1. Take one of the charts and cut out a small section of each colour.
2. Stick each small section on a different peg.
3. Mix the pegs in the container.
4. Lay out the other paint charts on a flat surface opposite the container.

Activity

Standing up, the children pull out a peg from the container and then attach it to the colour chart on the surface. Can they match all of the pegs before the time runs out?

Areas of development

• balance • hand-eye coordination • bi-lateral movement • crossing midline • proprioception • shoulder pivot • elbow pivot • wrist pivot • palm arches • pincer grip.

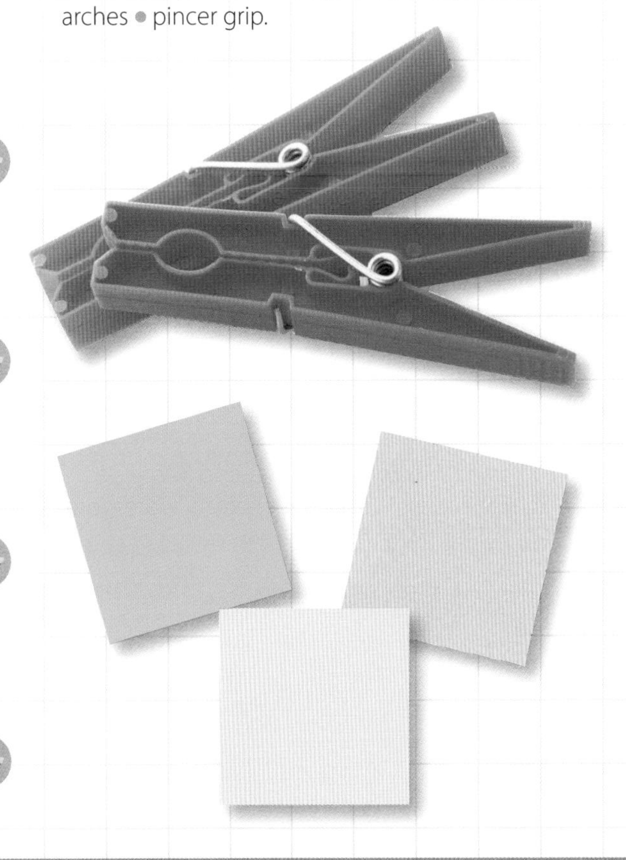

Dress to impress!

What you need

- Cartoon body cut out (any to suit the children's interests)
- Selection of clothes and accessories pre-cut
- Laminator and pouches
- Scissors

What to do

1. Print out the cartoon body onto card or paper and laminate it.
2. Print and cut out a selection of clothes and accessories that fit the body.
3. For more challenge, leave tabs on your cut outs for the children to fold over.
4. You can print out your images on magnetic printer paper to help everything stay in the right place!

Activity

Children 'dress' their cartoon body with various items in a variety of styles. For higher level engagement you could always put a photograph of the child's head on the top of the body.

Areas of development

• balance • hand-eye coordination • bi-lateral movement • crossing midline • proprioception • shoulder pivot • elbow pivot • wrist pivot • palm arches • pincer grip • knuckle pivot • PIP joint • DIP joint.

Pompom posting

What you need

- Various sizes of container with plastic lids
- Various sizes of pompoms
- Scissors
- Sharp pencil
- Tweezers

What to do

1. Use the pencil to puncture the plastic lid. This will help you to cut out holes.
2. Cut out a variety of different sized holes in each lid.
3. Mix the pompoms in a separate container.

Activity

Children use the tweezers to pick out a pompom and then post it through the appropriate hole in the lid of the container.

Areas of development

• hand-eye coordination • shoulder pivot • elbow pivot • wrist pivot • palm arches • pincer grip.

Lolly stick jigsaws

What you need

- Photographs or pictures
- PVA glue
- Scissors
- Lolly sticks

What to do

1. Put a layer of glue on the back of the photographs or pictures.
2. Stick two lolly sticks to the back of the picture a little bit apart.
3. Leave to dry.
4. Turn over and carefully cut in between the lolly sticks.

Activity

Mix up the lolly sticks and get the children to remake the picture. Use more sticks or thinner sticks for greater challenge.

Areas of development

• hand-eye coordination • elbow pivot • wrist pivot • palm arches • pincer gri • knuckle pivot.

Tin foil cars

What you need

- Scissors
- Tin foil
- Toy cars

What to do

1. Cut the tin foil into rectangles large enough to cover the cars that you are using.

Activity

The children lay the tin foil over their chosen car (making sure their car is in the middle) and then smooth it down all over (except the bottom) to create an exact imprint. Remove the car and trim around the foil replica.

Areas of development

• hand-eye coordination • bi-lateral movement • elbow pivot • wrist pivot • palm arches • pincer grip • knuckle pivot • PIP joint • DIP joint.

Cardboard tube toss

What you need

- A4 sheet of thin card
- Lots of paperclips
- Sticky tape

What to do

1. Roll the card onto itself to form a cylinder.
2. Secure with a paperclip at each end.
3. Seal the seam with sticky tape.

Activity

Children put paperclips next to each other around the perimeter of one of the ends of the cylinder. Once all of the paperclips are in place the children toss their tube in the air and watch it fly. For a smaller version children could use a ready-made cardboard inner tube.

Areas of development

• balance • hand-eye coordination • bi-lateral movement • crossing midline • proprioception • shoulder pivot • elbow pivot • wrist pivot • palm arches • pincer grip • knuckle pivot • PIP joint • DIP joint

Lollipop and ear bud bow and arrow

What you need

- Sharp knife
- Large lollipop sticks
- Ear buds
- Dental floss
- Scissors

What to do

1. Use the knife (adult only) to put a notch at each side of the top of the lollipop stick 1 cm from the end.
2. Repeat at the other end of the stick.
3. Wrap the dental floss several times around one end of the stick making sure it goes into your notches.
4. Do not cut the floss and repeat at the other end of the stick, bending the stick slightly before you wrap the floss.
5. Cut one of the cotton wool ends off an ear bud, leaving the other in tact.

Activity

Children use a pincer grip with one hand to hold the bow while using the other to fire their cotton bud arrow.

Areas of development

• balance • hand-eye coordination • bi-lateral movement • elbow pivot • wrist pivot • palm arches • pincer grip • knuckle pivot • PIP joint • DIP joint.

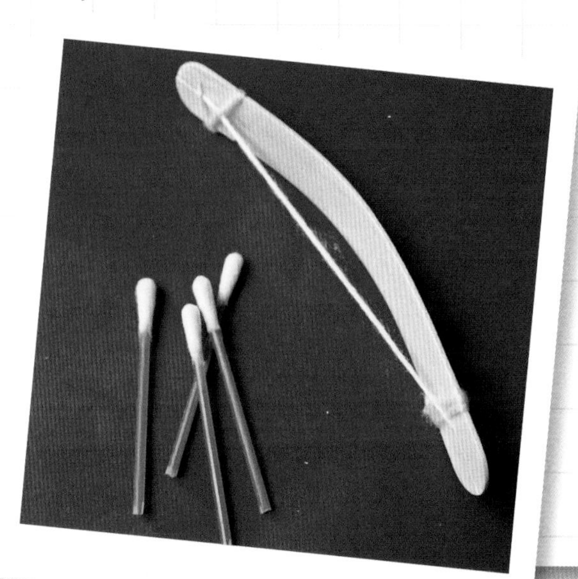

Drinking straw aeroplane

What you need

- Drinking straws
- A4 paper
- Sticky tape

What to do

1. Cut one strip of paper, 2.5 cm wide and 12.5 cm long.
2. Cut another piece of paper 2.5 cm wide and 25 cm long.
3. Loop each strip around to form a circle and attach with sticky tape.
4. Attach one paper circle to each end of your straw.

Activity

Children use their upper body, strength and balance to throw their 'aeroplanes' high and hard!

Areas of development

• balance • hand-eye coordination • bi-lateral movement • crossing midline • proprioception • shoulder pivot • elbow pivot • wrist pivot • palm arches • pincer grip.

Bottle top blaster

What you need

- Scissors
- 1 litre plastic bottle
- Balloons
- Pompoms (or other appropriate 'missiles' to fire)

What to do

1. Cut the top third from the bottle to create a funnel.
2. Put the neck of the balloon over the mouth of the bottle.

Activity

Children put their pompom (or other missile) into their bottle funnel. They hold the neck of the bottle with one hand while pulling back hard and releasing the balloon with the other. Their missile will be fired for some distance.

Areas of development

• balance • hand-eye coordination • bi-lateral movement • proprioception • elbow pivot • wrist pivot • palm arches • pincer grip • knuckle pivot • PIP joint • DIP joint.

Hammer art

What you need

- Flowers and leaves
- Watercolour paper
- Kitchen paper
- Hammer
- Tweezers

What to do

1. Collect flowers and leaves.
2. Separate kitchen towel into individual sheets.

Activity

Children lay the flowers and leaves onto the watercolour paper and cover with a sheet of kitchen towel. Using the hammer the children hit the kitchen paper until they can begin to see the flowers and leaves showing through.

Areas of development

• balance • hand-eye coordination • bi-lateral movement • crossing midline • proprioception • shoulder pivot • elbow pivot • wrist pivot • palm arches • pincer grip • knuckle pivot • PIP joint • DIP joint.

Sugar shakers and cocktail sticks

What you need

- Sugar shaker
- Cocktail sticks or spaghetti
- Tweezers (optional)
- Timer

What to do

1. Leave the cocktail sticks in their small container (beware sharp ends).
2. Get the children to snap the spaghetti in half to make it more manageable.

Activity

Children can use their finger or tweezers to pick up the cocktail sticks or spaghetti and push them through the holes in the top of the sugar shaker. The challenge is to get as many as they can into the jar in the time available.

Areas of development

• hand-eye coordination • elbow pivot, • wrist pivot, palm arches • pincer grip • knuckle pivot.

Locks and keys
(tinker table)

What you need

- Different sized locks (available form hardware and DIY shops)
- Matching keys
- Timer

What to do

1. Lock the locks.
2. Mix up the keys.

Activity

Children must sort through the keys to find the ones that will open the locks and to match as many as they can in the time given.

Areas of development

• hand-eye coordination • bi-lateral movement • wrist pivot • palm arches • pincer grip • knuckle pivot • PIP joint • DIP joint.

Moving water

What you need

- Water
- Two containers
- Food colouring (optional)
- Drinking straw

What to do

1. Fill one container with water and place at one side of the table.
2. Place the empty container at the other side.

Activity

A child stands in between the two containers. First of all they take a straw and dip it into the container with water in it. Once the end of the straw is under the water they have to block the other end of the straw with their thumb. When they lift the straw out there will be some water trapped in it. Next they reach across and put the straw into the empty pot and remove their thumb. At this point the water will come out. How much water can they move in the time that they have got?

Areas of development

• balance, hand-eye coordination • bi-lateral movement • crossing midline • proprioception • shoulder pivot • elbow pivot • wrist pivot • palm arches • knuckle pivot • PIP joint.

Freezer bag maze

What you need

- Zip lock freezer bag
- Duct tape
- Marble
- Liquid soap or washing-up liquid

What to do

1. Cut the duct tape into different lengths.
2. Fold it back on itself to form tubes of tape with the sticky side out.
3. Stick these tubes inside the freezer bag starting at the bottom.
4. Leave some gaps in between.
5. Squeeze the soap into the bag.
6. Add a marble.

Activity

By manipulating the contents of the bag, children try to push the marble through the soapy maze using their fingers.

Areas of development

• hand-eye coordination • wrist pivot • palm arches • knuckle pivot • PIP joint.

Lollipop stick and Velcro construction

What you need

- Large and small lollipop sticks
- Self adhesive Velcro

What to do

1. Stick a piece of Velcro to the ends and middle of the lollipop sticks.

Activity

Children use the different sized sticks to create a variety of models. Their skill development will be dependent on the size of their model.

Areas of development

• balance • hand-eye coordination • bi-lateral movement • crossing midline • proprioception • shoulder pivot • elbow pivot • wrist pivot • palm arches • pincer grip • knuckle pivot • PIP joint • DIP joint.

Chapter 8

Malleable materials activities and recipes

organised by skill level

1: Emergent skill

2: Developing skill

3: Advanced skill

1: Emergent skill

Tapioca

You will need:

- Packet of dry tapioca
- Warm water
- Food colouring

Method:

1. Roll the tapioca under your hands.
2. Add warm water to the uncooked tapioca and it will thicken.

Clean mud

You will need:

- 1 bar of white soap
- Cheese grater
- 1 roll white toilet paper
- Hot water
- Utensils for mixing

Method:

1. Shred the toilet paper into the water tray.
2. Grate the soap on top of the shredded paper and then mix with hands.
3. Slowly pour in hot water (the water must be hot enough to melt the soap but not too hot to cause a safety hazard).
4. Mix with utensils while the water is still hot.
5. When a little cooler mix with hands.

Cloud dough

You will need:

- 5 cups of plain flour
- 1 cup of baby oil
- Glitter (optional)
- Food colouring (optional)

Method:

1. Stir the oil into the flour.
2. Add the glitter and/or food colouring.

Porridge goo

You will need:

- Porridge oats
- Warm water
- Food colouring/powder paint

Method:

1. Put the dry oats into a large tray and let the children experience, touch and play with them first.
2. Add warm water a little at a time and get the children to mix it in with their fingers.
3. Add food colouring or powder paint toifferent parts of the tray and mix with fingers.

Puffed-up soap

You will need:

- I cup of grated soap (white)
- ¾ cup of warm water
- Food colouring
- Zip lock freezer bag

Method:

1. Slowly add the water to the grated soap.
2. Stir gently, otherwise you will get bubbles – you are aiming for a thick paste.
3. Spoon the paste into zip lock bags.
4. Add a few drops of food colouring to each bag and let the children squash until it's mixed in!
5. Snip the corner off the bag and squeeze away (start with a small snip – you can always make it bigger if you need to).
6. Use hands to spread the puffed-up soap.

Jelly

You will need:

- Jelly cubes or crystals
- Warm water
- Different-sized plastic containers
- Ice cube tray
- Rubber/plastic gloves
- Plastic bags
- A selection of small interesting objects (jewels, creepy crawlies)

Method:

1. Mix up the jelly as per the instructions on the packet.
2. Pour into a number of different-sized containers.
3. You could use a plastic glove for a jelly handshake! (You will have to cut the glove off once the jelly has set.)
4. For a different sensory experience, pour some liquid jelly into a sealable plastic bag.
5. Add any other 'objects' to your jelly at the liquid stage.
6. When the jelly is set, let the children tip it out of the moulds onto a large surface and get stuck in.

Edible finger paint

You will need:

- 2 cups of cornflour
- 1 cup of cold water
- 4½ cups of boiling water
- Food colouring

Method:

1. Mix the cornflour with the cold water and stir together.
2. Pour in the boiling water (adult only) and stir between each cup.
3. Keep stirring!
4. When it becomes like the consistency of thick custard it's done.
5. Add food colouring as required.

Marshmallow slime

You will need:

- Bag of marshmallows
- Food colouring
- Washing-up liquid

Method:

1. Heat the marshmallows in the pan or microwave until they begin to melt and become sticky (be careful not to overheat and burn).
2. Add a good squirt of washing-up liquid to make the marshmallows sticky and slimy.
3. Add food colouring.

Smells yummy!

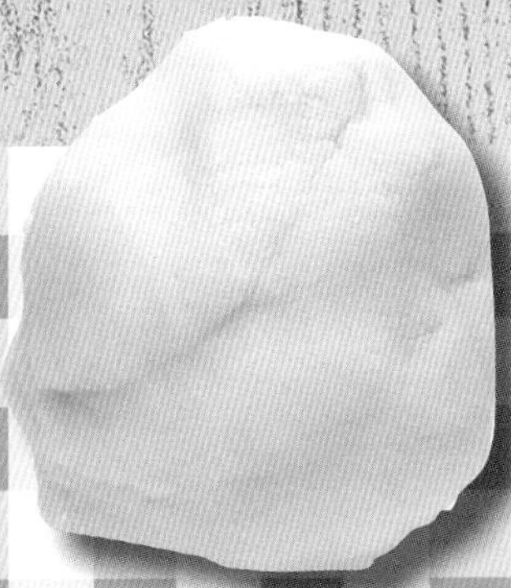

COOKED

Basic dough recipe

You will need:

- 1 cup flour
- ½ cup salt
- 1 cup water
- 2 tbs oil
- 2 tbs cream of tartar

Method:

1. Mix flour, salt and oil, and slowly add the water.
2. Cook over medium heat, stirring until dough becomes stiff.
3. Turn out onto wax paper and let cool.
4. Knead the play dough with your hands until of appropriate consistency.

NOT COOKED

Basic dough recipe

You will need:

- 2 cups plain flour (all purpose)
- 2 tbs vegetable oil
- ½ cup salt
- 2 tbs cream of tartar
- Up to 2 cups boiling water
- Few drops of glycerine

Method:

1. Mix the flour, salt, cream of tartar and oil in a large mixing bowl.
2. Add the boiling water.
3. Stir continuously until it becomes a sticky, combined dough.
4. Add the food glycerine to make it shiny (optional).
5. Allow it to cool down then take it out of the bowl and knead it quickly until all of the stickiness has gone.

For these recipes follow the instructions for the uncooked dough (page 55) then add the dry ingredients when you add the flour to your dough.

Chocolate dough

You will also need

- 1 cup cocoa powder

Method

1. Add the cocoa powder with the rest of the dry ingredients.
2. You can also add chocolate chips or vermicelli to your dough for added texture.
3. If you are going to add real chocolate, wait until the dough has cooled and then knead in.

Cinnamon dough

You will also need

- 1 tbs of dried cinnamon

Method

1. Add the cinnamon with the rest of the dry ingredients and mix well.
2. For an extra spicy twist to this dough you can add other spice such as nutmeg.
3. Get the children to crush spices in a pestle and mortar or grate nutmeg as part of the process.

For these recipes follow the instructions for the uncooked dough (page 55) then add the extra ingredients when your dough has cooled.

Flower petal dough

You will also need

- 3 or 4 cups of flower petals
- Food colouring (optional)

Method

1. Slowly knead in the flower petals once the dough has cooled. If the dough is too hot then they will go sticky and discolour.

Herb dough

You will also need

- Large bunch of fresh herbs

Method

1. Shred the herbs with your hands and then add to the cool dough, knead until they are all mixed in.

Lavender dough

You will also need

- 2 tbs of dried or fresh lavender
- 2 drops of lavender oil (optional)
- Purple food colouring (optional)

Method

1. Mix the dry lavender in with the other dry ingredients.
2. Add the lavender oil and purple food colouring with the the water and stir well.
3. For added texture you can knead in lavender flowers once the dough has been formed.

For these recipes follow the instructions for the uncooked dough (page 55) then add the extra ingredients when your dough has cooled.

Fruit dough

You will also need

- 1 sachet of powdered fruit flavouring

Method

1. Add the fruit flavouring with the flour.

Jelly dough

You will also need

- 1 packet of jelly crystals

Method

1. Add the jelly crystals with the flour.

Sparkle dough

You will also need

- 1 cup of glitter

Method

1. Add glitter to the dough when it has cooled, kneading it to mix through.

Sand dough

You will also need

- 1 cup of sand

Method

1. Add sand to the kneaded dough when it has cooled.

For these recipes follow the instructions for the uncooked dough (page 55) then add the liquid with the boiling water.

Beetroot play dough

You will also need

- Beetroot

Method

1. Chop up one medium sized beetroot and put in pan with a cup of water. Bring to the boil then gently simmer on a stove for ten minutes. Once cooled pour through sieve.
2. Follow the uncooked playdough recipe replacing 1 cup of boiling water with the beetroot liquid.

Raspberry dough

You will also need

- 12 raspberries (approx.)

Method

1. Put a big handful of raspberries and a cup of water in a pan. Bring to the boil then gently simmer on stove for 20 minutes (until liquid has reduced to about half). Once cooled pour through sieve then follow the playdough recipe adding the raspberry liquid at stage 2 with 1 cup boiling water.

Tree bark dough

You will also need

- Tree bark

Method

1. Put a big handful of tree bark in a pan with a cup of water (it's best not to take it directly from the tree – if you scout around you will find plenty on the ground). Bring to the boil then gently simmer on stove for 20-30 minutes (until liquid has reduced to about half). Once cooled pour through sieve.
2. Follow the uncooked playdough recipe replacing 1 cup of boiling water with 1 cup of bark liquid.

Salt dough

You will need

- 1 cup of flour
- 1 cup of salt
- ½ cup of water

Method

1. Mix all of the ingredients together.
2. Knead the dough on a flat surface until it becomes workable.
3. You can harden the dough by cooking on a baking sheet in the oven at 100° C/ 200° F for two to three hours.

Porridge dough

You will need

- 2 cups plain flour (all purpose)
- I cup of porridge oats
- 2 tbs vegetable oil
- 1 tbs honey
- ½ cup salt
- 2 tbs cream of tartar
- Up to 2 cups boiling water
- Few drops glycerine

Method

1. Mix the flour, salt, porridge oats, cream of tartar and oil in a large mixing bowl.
2. Add the boiling water and honey.
3. Stir continuously until it becomes a sticky, combined dough.
4. Add the food glycerine to make it shiny (optional).
5. Allow it to cool down then take it out of the bowl and knead it quickly until all of the stickiness has gone.

Marshmallow playdough

You will need

- 4 to 5 cups of marshmallows
- 2 tbs water
- 2 tbs cooking oil
- 4 to 5 cups of cornflour

Method

1. Melt the marshmallows and the water in a pan over a medium heat.
2. Remove from the heat and add the oil.
3. Stir in four to five cups of cornflour slowly.
4. Keep stirring until you get a pliable mixture.
5. If it is too sticky, add more cornflour.

Sand mousse

You will need

- Play sand
- Washing-up liquid
- Water

Method

1. Make a well in the middle of the sand.
2. Slowly pour in the water.
3. Add a squirt of washing-up liquid.
4. The quantities depend on how much mousse you want. Half of the fun is adding different amounts of the ingredients as you go along to get the desired effect.

Bread dough

You will need

- 450 g strong white bread flour
- 1 tsp salt
- 2 tsp dried easy blend yeast
- 300 ml water (that has been boiled)
- 2 tbs oil

Method

1. Sift flour and salt into a bowl and then add yeast.
2. Slowly stir in the warm water and oil with a wooden spoon to make a dough.
3. Put the dough onto a clean surface and knead thoroughly for about ten minutes.

Fruit putty

You will need

- 1 packet of crystalised or powdered jelly
- 2 cups of flour
- 1 cup of salt
- 4 tbs cream of tartar
- 2 tbs cooking oil
- 2 cups of boiling water
- A pan
- Heat source to heat the pan

Method

1. Mix all the dry ingredients together in a pan.
2. Add the boiling water and stir.
3. Heat the pan and keep stirring until the ingredients come together to form a ball.

Soap flake mini cakes

You will need

- 1 box of soap flakes
- Water

Method

1. Add water to the soap flakes and stir gently until you have the consistency of double cream.
2. Pour into small shallow containers and leave to set. (How long this process takes depends on how thick your pancake is.)
3. Turn out your rubbery pancake into your tray and begin to explore.

Sand putty

You will need

- 2 cups of sand
- 1 cup of cornflour
- PVA glue
- Food colouring

Method

1. Mix the cornflour and half a cup of PVA glue together.
2. Add the cornflour mix to two cups of sand.
3. Stir or mix with hands.
4. If it is too sticky add more sand. If it is too dry add more water.
5. Add food colouring if required.
6. Leave overnight.

(The starch in the cornflour removes the moisture from the glue leaving it more like a putty than a dough.)

Bread putty

You will need

- 1 slice of white bread (no crusts)
- 1 tablespoon of PVA glue
- Small bowl

Method

1. Rip up the bread into tiny pieces and put into the bowl.
2. Add the glue.
3. Get squidging with your fingers.
4. Keep going until you have a sticky dough-like consistency.

Rubbery dough

You will need

- 2 cups baking powder
- 1½ cups water
- 1 cup cornflour
- A pan
- Heat source to heat the pan

Method

1. Mix with a fork until smooth. Boil over medium heat until thick. Spoon onto plate or wax paper.

Water beads

You will need

- Packs of water beads
- Water

Method

1. Soak the beads overnight then allow the children to break them apart and examine the contents.